SWISS NEUTRALITY

SWISS NEUTRALITY

Its History and Meaning

by

EDGAR BONJOUR

Professor of History
at the University of Basle

TRANSLATED BY
MARY HOTTINGER

LONDON

GEORGE ALLEN & UNWIN LTD

MUSEUM STREET

FIRST PUBLISHED IN GREAT BRITAIN IN 1946
SECOND IMPRESSION 1948
SECOND EDITION (THIRD IMPRESSION) 1952

PRINTED IN GREAT BRITAIN
in 11-pt. Baskerville type
BY JARROLD AND SONS LIMITED, NORWICH

CONTENTS

INTRODUCTION

UP TO A generation ago, the Swiss citizen lived with a
feeling of security in foreign relations which we can
hardly credit today. Neutrality had come to be taken so
much for granted as the fundamental principle of the
Federal constitution, and had been so generally recognized
in Europe, that it seemed unthreatened and even
inviolable. It blended with the republican and democratic ideal to form a national myth of almost religious
sanctity. As the axiom of Swiss foreign policy, it had
certainly suffered attack both in theory and in fact, but
since such crises had always been successfully overcome,
Switzerland's faith in the inviolability of her neutrality
had merely been confirmed. It was as if the country
were girdled with high, protecting ramparts, behind
which its people could go about their lawful occasions
unmolested. It was during this period of calm in Switzerland's foreign relations that international law assiduously
sought a formula for the theory of neutrality.

The outbreak of the first world war in 1914 brought a
rude awakening from such illusions. Not only did the
belligerents override temporary declarations of neutrality,
but ancient charters of neutrality, guaranteeing its
permanence, became mere scraps of paper. This was
made painfully clear by the violation of Belgian neutrality. Theoretical speculation dissolved like mist in a
cruel and naked reality, and all that remained was the
anxious and fateful question whether neutrality could be
preserved and the integrity of the native soil maintained.
When, however, Switzerland had been able to preserve
her neutrality intact throughout the war, when she was
able to anchor her permanent neutrality in the international covenants of the League of Nations, the old

feeling of security returned almost unabated. Under pressure from the great Powers, she had, it is true, been obliged to restrict her integral to a differential neutrality. Not without grave misgivings, she found herself ousted from her traditional, total neutrality, and it was only in order to avoid exclusion from the general reorganization of international law that, reluctantly enough, she agreed to surrender part of her neutrality and thenceforth to take her part in the economic sanctions of the League. As long as the covenant of world peace seemed intact, Switzerland could feel secure, but the more the ties of the new family of nations relaxed, the less the minor states could expect from its protection, and the more urgent were Switzerland's efforts to cast off the fetters of a differential neutrality and to resume the axiom of her foreign policy in its traditional form.

Not long before the outbreak of the second world war, the Confederation had regained its traditional, that is its " strict and total " neutrality. With that, any possible misconception of her international attitude and international status was obviated. When the general order of peace broke down, Switzerland was in no way involved in the world struggle by treaty obligations to any power. The collapse of international law brought painfully home to her how well she had done to place no reliance on written assurances, but only on her own will and her own strength. It was the fact that neutrality had brought the Confederation through the last huge conflagration with its national independence unviolated and its territory intact which finally impressed the rightness of its traditional principle in foreign policy deep on the Swiss national consciousness.

In the post-war period, with its international conflicts and tensions, and world war still a threat, the Swiss abide by their belief that the neutrality and inviolability of the Confederation are in the true interests of Europe as a whole and an indispensable factor in international relations. But in high politics it does not matter much what small countries regard as being in or contrary to the interests of Europe as a whole ; that is, of its nature, a matter for the great Powers to decide. In the public opinion of the world, the understanding of Swiss neutrality seems to be on the decline, as recent discussions have shown. Unjust judgments have been passed on it. They are to be regarded in part as a product of the war of ideologies, the universal conflict which has at all times tended to regard the very principle of neutrality with hostility. The recent opposition to neutrality, however, arises from a movement which, starting from a new conception of international organization, outlaws war as an instrument of national power politics. What is often overlooked is that the traditional principle of Swiss foreign policy lies in the very nature of the Confederation, that neutrality is an essential element of Swiss democracy and a bulwark of Swiss freedom, and indeed that it is on neutrality that the existence of Switzerland as a nation is founded.

Further, it is not realized that, as several hundred years of experience have shown, Swiss neutrality is a factor of security in the vicissitudes of international politics. There is hardly another country whose foreign policy has such a permanent feature to show.

The aim of the present essay is to give some insight into these matters and to contribute to a deeper grasp and a more unbiased appreciation of Swiss neutrality, based on the facts of history.

Chapter 1

ORIGIN AND GROWTH OF SWISS NEUTRALITY

The absolute neutrality of Switzerland as a political principle is generally dated from the year 1674, when the Federal Diet declared that the Confederation, as a body, would regard itself as a neutral state and intervene on neither side in the war which had just broken out. In this way the Confederation proclaimed the axiom of its foreign policy to the forum of Europe. It must not, however, be assumed that the fundamental principle of Swiss political life was then established by a single voluntary act. On the contrary, the principle of neutrality had emerged very slowly from the treaty policy of the old Confederation, and awakened only gradually to a realization of its own nature out of the limbo of international entanglements. It had taken two hundred years of painful experience for the Confederation to grasp its own vital necessities, for the policy of expansion to be abandoned and Switzerland trained in the political abstinence of neutrality. And for a long time to come it remained an elastic formula, in which the most manifold aspects of abstinence in foreign policy found what may be called a national expression.

It is unnecessary at this point to provide a list of written statements of neutrality in the early history of the Swiss Leagues, though the list would be surprisingly long. Neutrality in the policy both of single members of the Confederation, and of the Confederation as a whole, can be traced back almost to its foundation. The idea of Swiss neutrality is actually almost coeval with the idea of a Swiss nation. There are instances in plenty to show that not only in mediaeval times, but quite particularly in the transition from medieval to modern history, the idea of neutrality was officially known to the Confederation. In

Swiss records we first encounter it denoted by the German word " stillesitzen," to sit still. The term " neutralitet " first occurs in 1536. The use of this foreign word which, being derived from Low Latin, was internationally intelligible, first became customary in Switzerland in the course of the 17th century.

Research into the origins of neutrality in foreign affairs brings to light a whole group of causes. In the following discussion the order in which they are presented is no indication of their order of importance in the development of neutrality.

It has always been the custom to date Swiss neutrality from the battle of Marignano. That great defeat, it is argued, checked further expansion on the part of the Confederation, whereupon it took refuge in neutrality. There is a certain truth in the argument, since it was actually the collapse of its highly expansive power policy which threw the Confederation back upon itself. That must not be taken to mean that its strength was broken, and that it was converted to abstinence in foreign policy at one blow. The Confederation continued to give proof in plenty of its overflowing vitality and linked its cause to that of princes. But the resistance it encountered and the defeats it suffered abroad checked the course of its reckless militarism and compelled it to take thought.

Many Swiss then realized that so loose a congeries of states, so half-baked a political organization as the Confederation was at that time, did not possess the necessary strength either for a uniform foreign policy or for clear-cut military aims. Their experiences in Italy had taught them a bloody lesson. Any advance in that direction implied one step, the centralization of the Confederation. Every state which has entered on the path of power in foreign policy has first had to go the way of internal union, whether it be France at the time of the Revolution or the dictator states of today. But for the

Confederation, at the end of the Middle Ages, it meant the surrender of its cardinal constitutional principle, namely, federation ; it meant the sacrifice of regional and communal autonomy ; in a word, the abandonment of everything that bore the name of Swiss. At that time a solution of the kind seemed as impossible as it had done at the end of the previous century, when the federal order triumphed in the Compact of Stans. It was for the sake of the federal state that the Confederation abandoned its policy of aggression and approximated to the political principle of neutrality at a time when other countries were turning their energies outward in wars of conquest or adventuring on the high seas to open up far-distant lands. In their Swiss forms, there is a secret affinity between freedom and neutrality. Not that the motive here put forward had by that time become fully conscious. The majority had but a vague notion of the ultimate motives of their actions and the connection between them.

The religious cleavage had at least as great an influence on the development of the idea of neutrality as the collapse of the policy of power. We know how the religious conflict accentuated the existing territorial chaos and undermined the national cohesion of the Confederation, till Switzerland almost ceased to exist as a living organism. This internal disintegration could not but contribute to the paralysis of any external action. The two faiths lived in a reciprocally neutralizing equilibrium. Since each took up the cause of its co-religionists abroad, it thwarted the aims of its Swiss countrymen. Had one religious party taken up arms for one religion in Europe, the other would have immediately followed suit. The result would have been a devastating expansion of the European crisis on to the territory of the Confederation. This in its turn would have brought about the disruption of Switzerland and hence threatened her national existence with destruction.

From the outset there was no lack of attempts to draw the Confederation into the European wars of religion. Foreign potentates and certain Swiss of both creeds furthered such aims, but in the end, political common sense always succeeded in averting the ultimate disaster. The Confederation held aloof from the wars of religion both in the 16th and the 17th centuries. When Gustavus Adolphus of Sweden sought a religious alliance with the Swiss protestants, there was a party in Zurich which was more than ready to meet him halfway But although individuals were passionately in favour of the alliance, the government returned a negative answer.

Later, when the religious strife in Europe had somewhat abated and had ceased to provoke wars, Switzerland was slow to go the same way. Even at the beginning of the 18th century, in the dawn of the Enlightenment, outside observers were surprised to note that both home and foreign policy were still determined by the religious conflict. But ultimately, even the religious division lost its edge. What remained ineffaceable was the cultural and intellectual antagonism born of the difference in religion. Owing to that difference, two distinct national types have developed, whose features are still clearly distinguishable. Protestant Switzerland continued to remain in close touch with protestant Europe. We have only to think of the wealth of relations in every sphere of life between the protestant cantons and protestant Germany as well as England, Calvinist Holland, the Huguenot parts of France, and protestant Poland. Catholic Switzerland remained in contact with catholic Europe, with France, Spain, certain Italian states and the catholic territories of the old German Empire, and here too, the old community of faith, transcending national frontiers, proved fruitful in its results. It was in this way that the cultural cleavage in Europe was carried into Switzerland. If these two divergent currents were to be blended in one

14

political whole, they must of necessity adopt neutrality as the axiom of their foreign policy. Neutrality was, it is true, powerless to fuse the conflicting forces, the almost countless local peculiarities, of the Confederation in one creative whole, but it prevented a disruption of the Confederation, which would have meant political dissolution.

The fact that the Confederation was composed of different racial and linguistic groups had no effect whatever on the development on neutrality. For at the time of which we are speaking, Switzerland was officially of Germanic race and Germanic tongue throughout. It was not until the second half of the 19th century, in the period of the rise of national power states, that the component elements of the country began to become aware of a kinship with neighbouring cultures, an awareness which, as we well know, proved to be a surprisingly disruptive force in the first world war. This recent development, which was not foreseen by former generations, has imparted a new meaning to the idea of neutrality and engendered new forces of union. Thus here too, the heritage of the fathers has proved a blessing to the sons.

The treaty system of the Confederation was also of such a nature as to force abstinence in foreign policy upon it. Both Switzerland as a whole and the various groups and members which composed it had entered into foreign alliances in all directions. In many cases, commitments ran counter to each other, and in case of war would necessarily have cancelled each other. In haphazard fashion, as each case arose, the Confederation had woven about itself a network of treaties which now threatened to enmesh it. If it had fully fulfilled every point in a single treaty, the threads which bound it on some other side would have snapped. This strange tangle, knotted by the need of protection and the spirit of gain, could hardly now be disentangled even by the experienced hands of the members of the Diet.

The most fateful involvement was that with France. It went back to the perpetual peace with Francis I of 1516 and the protective alliance of 1521. In these two treaties the Confederation committed itself to never permitting its soldiery to be used against the king of France and to closing the Alpine passes to his enemies. The king was further allowed to engage 6 to 16,000 mercenaries on Swiss territory, though they were only to be used for purposes of defence. In recognition of these concessions, the king undertook to send artillery and cavalry to the help of the Confederation if it should be attacked, and to pay considerable pensions to every member. Further, mutual economic preferences were agreed on, in which it must be admitted that Switzerland was the sole and great beneficiary. These agreements made the king of France the first friend of the Confederation. Nor did France ever take undue advantage of her privileged position, having a clear sense of her own interests. For if she had brought the Confederation into conflict with its other allies, it would have recalled the Swiss troops serving with the French forces, and hence deprived French foreign policy of one of its most potent weapons. It was for that reason that French diplomacy repeatedly intervened, often at the cost of great efforts, in order to prevent any interference in Swiss religious and political disputes, just as it was successful in restraining the Confederation from becoming too deeply involved in European quarrels. The rareness of civil war in Switzerland, in spite of acute internal tension, and the total absence of foreign wars, bear eloquent testimony to the skill of French secret diplomacy. By her ceaseless care for the peace of Switzerland, both at home and abroad, in the gravest crises, France not only did much to keep her alive, but also, though unwittingly, promoted the development of the idea of neutrality.

The omnipotent influence of France, which made itself felt into the finest ramifications of intellectual and cultural life, overshadowed that of the second great ally of the Confederation, the house of Hapsburg. The alliance between the Confederation and Austria was certainly older, and the Austrian diplomats did not fail to make good and skilful use of that argument to the Diet, which set great store by age and permanence. Yet for many reasons, that superb old museum piece, the Eternal Compact with Austria of 1511, lost much of its prestige. In that treaty the two signatories had promised not to allow their troops to take the field against each other and, should attack threaten, to keep vigilant watch. Later, the Alpine passes had to be kept open for Austria also. Not only this stipulation, but another concerning mercenaries were at variance with cardinal provisions in the French treaty. It was the Swiss statesmen's task to steer a course through these vaguenesses and inconsistencies.

Beside and across these, the strongest threads in the Swiss treaty system, individual cantons had formed alliances in many quarters. In 1577, although France objected, the catholic cantons concluded an alliance with the rising house of Savoy, and ten years later expanded the existing Capitulation of Milan into an alliance with Spain. Here too, promises were given of a supply of mercenary troops and the opening of the passes. These treaties had, it is true, been primarily aimed at the protestant Confederates, but they were also definitely hostile to France. On their side, the protestant Swiss entered into relations with the German protestants and with Venice. The relative positions of the partners to the treaty, however, shifted so radically after the revocation of the Edict of Nantes that the inner, catholic cantons became protégés of France. The Protestants, on the other hand, till that time the most loyal friends of France, sought contact with England under Cromwell and William of Orange, and even concluded a far-reaching military capitulation with Holland, one of Louis XIV's most bitter enemies.

The consistency with which the Confederation managed to find a practical way of reconciling incompatible written commitments, and sought the golden mean in the conflicts of the great powers, was a powerful factor in its education in neutrality. The Swiss were past-masters in appealing from one treaty to another and thus in playing off the members of the Confederation against each other. In confidential conversations, foreign ambassadors more than once expressed their admiration for the diplomatic skill of these peasants. From the national point of view, the involvement of the Confederation in the politics of the great Powers, and the rifts it caused at home, were certainly disastrous, yet it all turned out to the national advantage in the shape of neutrality.

The development of the balance of power in Europe coincides fairly exactly with the rise of Swiss neutrality. That is not fortuitous ; the equilibrium of the great Powers is actually an important presupposition of the Swiss policy of neutrality. As soon as the European family of states came to be regulated by the principle of equality, and not by that of predominance, though tensions were not relieved, Switzerland could feel secure. At all times the small have profited by the disputes of the great. The Confederation, the point at which the interests of the great Powers intersected as they did perhaps in no other small country, lived for a long time on the rivalry of its great neighbours. It might even be said that the balance of power born of the rivalry of the great Powers is the air in which the neutrality of the minor states thrives, while any ascendancy on the part of any one of them is the gravest threat to its existence. The neutrality of the state of Prussia-Brandenburg was also fostered by similar conditions, although in aim and essence it differed widely from that of the Confederation.

Swiss neutrality was intrinsically conservative, without ambitious schemes for the future, content with itself, consciously choosing a neutral attitude so that it might come unmolested through the strife of the great Powers ; Prussia-Brandenburg, on the contrary, restlessly progressive, pursued its policy of neutrality in order to secure the political and territorial expansion its rulers so eagerly coveted.

The entire history of the Confederation, from its origins to the present day, shows how consistent was the policy by which Switzerland sought to prevent the ascendancy of any one Power. She regularly joined the opponents of any Power aiming at hegemony. When, for instance, she sided with Charles V against Francis I in the famous imperial election of 1519, it was because the union of the crown of France with the imperial crown of Germany would have meant a far too dangerous conglomeration of power. In the following century she kept the friendship of Louis XIV until the growth of his power began to cast its shadow over Europe. But at that moment she began to turn an attentive ear to William of Orange's ideas on the balance of power, and English political thought found a striking response in Switzerland. The most impressive example of how mortally neutrality is affected by the predominance of any one power is given by the Napoleonic epoch. A harsh light is cast on the situation by Napoleon's remark : " *Vis-à-vis de moi, votre neutralité est un mot vide de sens.*" And later on it was not only radical resentment which actuated the young federal state in its hostility to Napoleon III, but the dawning suspicion of the possibility that he might rule the world. Swiss feeling about the dominant position of Germany under Bismarck is of the same nature.

The ascendancy of any single power, however, is not the only thing which threatens Swiss neutrality. Perfect harmony among them is equally dangerous. We can see this, for instance, in the post-Napoleonic period. The policy of the Holy Alliance led to infringements of Swiss sovereignty and a disregard of Swiss neutrality such as had only been experienced under Napoleon's protectorate. And finally, after the first world war of 1914-1918, the union of Europe in the League of Nations meant a restriction of Swiss neutrality.

Geographical conditions have also contributed to making neutrality the guiding principle of Swiss foreign policy. The Confederation, with its enviable and dominating key-position in the Alpine massif, situated in the heart of an over-populated Europe, in the midst of a crowd of jostling nations and exposed to their pressure, with partially open frontiers, its territory dove-tailed with that of so many restless neighbours, was faced with national perils which can only be compared with those threatening the German Empire. During the Thirty Years' War, the heritage of danger inseparable from a central position was demonstrated with great force to the Confederation by the inrush of alien powers on to German territory and its transformation into the theatre of the European struggle for power. The Confederation eluded the danger by girding on the armour of neutrality ; it did not completely cut Switzerland off from the outside world, but protected her from military embroilments.

Within the Confederation itself, certain members were bound to a form of neutrality established by treaty. From the beginning of the 16th century, every " state " joining the Confederation had to promise to " sit still " in case of civil war among the other members, that is, to assist neither side but to pave the way for negotiations. True to this promise, the members concerned held strictly aloof from participation in civil wars and sought, in some cases successfully, to restore peace. The part played by Basle in the home policy of the Confederation may actually be described as pacifist. A neutral attitude was always imposed on the common bailiwicks. This curious feature of Swiss federal policy contributed to the rise and preservation of Swiss neutrality as a whole. The old Swiss theory and practise of impartial arbitration in cases may also have worked to the same end.

Chapter 2

THE SCOPE OF SWISS NEUTRALITY

The conception of the scope and limitations of Swiss neutrality at the time of its origin and development differed markedly from that of today ; it may be described as looser, broader and vaguer. In order to obtain a precise idea of it, we must survey the earlier practise of neutrality as a whole, and deduce its essential features from that survey. For while the Diet took no pains to provide any clear definition of neutrality in its official pronouncements, international law, then in its infancy, did not remedy the defect. The members of the Diet certainly spoke from time to time of " traditional neutrality " as " the fundament of the Confederate Republic," or called neutrality " the pillar of its peace," but further definition was cautiously avoided. It is true that international lawyers of the time—Grotius in Holland or Emer de Vattel of Neuchatel, who was more familiar with conditions in Switzerland—sought to find a place for neutrality in their systems, but they did so quite superficially and the position of Switzerland was merely alluded to. Practice hastened ahead of theory. It is notable that the Swiss practice of neutrality was governed by stricter principles than its doctrine in international law, and indeed the idea of a more absolute neutrality was first conceived and put into practice in Switzerland. We may even regard the development of the idea of absolute neutrality as a specifically Swiss contribution to European international law.

One essential difference between early neutrality and that of today lies in mercenary service. On the whole, under the *ancien régime* there was no objection to Switzerland supplying troops to foreign powers in spite of her neutrality, and even after 1815, that is, after the international recognition of her permanent neutrality, Switzerland had no hesitation in concluding military capitulations with foreign powers. It took quite different arguments, the rise of industry and the ideology of radicalism, to cast public discredit on mercenary service and abolish the military capitulations with other countries. At a time when the national army was hardly known, when most wars were fought with hired troops, the Swiss export of mercenaries was looked on far more as a matter of course. The fact that foreign mercenary service was an absolute economic necessity for a country so over-populated as Switzerland was only ignored by theologians like Zwingli, whose minds were ruled by general ideas, or by Utopists like Sir Thomas More, who speculated on what ought to be and not on what was. In his Utopia, More held up to scorn the mercenary people of the Zapoletes, that is, the Swiss, with a touch of the somewhat summary moral arrogance of the Erasmian pacifist. Otherwise the only voices raised against mercenary service were those of individual foreigners who had had little or no success in enlisting the military power of the Confederation. As a general rule, Europe was glad that Switzerland supplied troops at all, and took good care, on that account, not to brand mercenary service as unneutral.

It was, of course, a condition that Switzerland should grant the right to engage mercenaries equally to all parties applying for it. From the outset, the Swiss established equality of treatment of all as a principle to be shaken neither by threats nor promises. When France attempted to monopolize the recruitment of the Swiss troops, and would not allow Switzerland to supply troops to her enemies, there was an unwonted unanimity in the Swiss refusal to admit such an infringement of Swiss sovereignty. Other countries always supported

Switzerland in her belief in the rightness of this view. Thus, in the old Confederation the position was that Switzerland could uphold her neutrality not in spite of the supply of troops to foreign countries, but because of it. The export of soldiers was even the condition on which Europe granted to Switzerland her privileged position as a neutral country.

It took a harder struggle for the idea of territorial neutrality to be generally accepted. According to the agreements undertaken, France and Hapsburg Spain had the right to use the Swiss passes for military transit. It was clear that such transits meant the gravest threat to Swiss neutrality. Every time the passage of foreign armies came up for discussion in the Diet, feeling ran high. In the practise of granting the right of passage, the Confederation could appeal to the authority of the most famous international lawyer of the time. In his work *De jure belli ac pacis*, published in 1625, Hugo Grotius upheld the right of transit in all circumstances. He did not admit any grounds of refusal by the neutrals, not even their fear of the military power of the army in transit. The unhappy experiences of the Confederation in the Thirty Years' War, however, led to a unanimous resolution by catholics and protestants " to grant to none the right of passage through Swiss territory, and to prevent anyone from so doing with all their might." Therewith the Swiss dissociated themselves from the theory of the harmlessness of military transit upheld by international law. In the succeeding years they continued to abide by the stricter principle.

After the Peace of Münster the general prohibition of free passage was already a *fait accompli* in Switzerland. If this rigour was shown to their own allies, they could hardly be more lax with other countries. The inviolability of neutral territory, and the clearly expressed determination to defend it with armed force, were now sufficient to warn foreign armies off. Slight violations of territory at Basle were in themselves insignificant, but the loud and bitter complaints provoked by such trifles testified to the heightening of Swiss awareness of territorial violations. Respect for the neutrality of Swiss territory had grown everywhere. If we trace the violations of Swiss territory from the 16th to the 18th century on a map, we shall realize that they were mere frontier scratches. Foreign armies never crossed Switzerland, nor did they make Swiss territory their theatre of war, as happened later at the time of the French Revolution and Napoleon.

In the theory and practice of economic neutrality, curious fluctuations may be observed in the course of time. One is even tempted to regard the older practice as stricter. Grotius gives us no help at this point, although it is just here that the increase in international traffic would have required clearer definitions. Thus the Confederation had perforce to fall back on its own judgment. On principle, the Diet prohibited the supply of arms and munitions to other countries, though as a rule foreign armies might revictual themselves in Switzerland. Here too, however, care was taken that all parties should be treated as equally as possible. The Diet always admitted the right of individual foreign soldiers to buy in Swiss markets. It also allowed practically every army operating near the frontiers to buy provisions in order to gain their good will and thus, as far as might be, avert danger from the frontiers. In practice, it does not seem to have drawn any very clear distinction as to whether the victuals were supplied by private persons or by the individual cantonal governments. The lack of personnel for purposes of control prevented strict supervision ; indeed the state had not, at that time, assumed control of all branches of economic life. The well-stocked markets of Switzerland and her practice of free trading were among the reasons why the belligerents supported Swiss neutrality.

In the old Confederation, neutrality in the public expression of opinion was practically unknown. That neutrality must not be taken to mean indifference to events in the political world, which has never existed in Switzerland at any time. What is meant by it is voluntary abstention from any passionate partisanship, the intention to do justice, the effort to approach even men of other race with understanding. Such an attitude is to be found neither among governors nor governed in earlier times. The old Swiss were violent partisans and expressed their feelings without restraint. They did so by word of mouth in the guildhouse or the tavern, where they met in small circles to discuss world events. On a bigger scale, they discussed the position at fairs or markets, where they met their countrymen from the remoter districts and argued with men of different mind. Not even in the *Landsgemeinde* or the Council Hall was there any restraint. In every part of the country we find not only a French and an Austrian party, but even Spanish, Savoyard, Dutch and Venetian parties. Individual families would declare themselves the hereditary supporters of some great power or other, and stuck to their colours. Or again, great military leaders would become popular. Thus during the war of the Spanish Succession, Berne celebrated the exploits of Marlborough with as much jubilation as if they had been her own, while in the war of the Austrian Succession, the great hero was Frederick II. The battles of opinion in Switzerland were often mere echoes of European conflicts ; for want of great subjects of dispute at home, parochial politics were seasoned with foreign salt.

The free expression of opinion in print was more difficult, at any rate as far as the newspapers were concerned. For the newspapers were under the supervision of the governments and often their mouthpiece. They were mere conveyers of information, not party organs. Hence there was as yet no so-called public opinion manipulated by the press. The defect was made good by the orgy of pamphleteering. The small pamphlet was the great instrument in the struggle for the public opinion of Switzerland. The mountains of literature of this kind produced at various times and preserved in cantonal and foreign archives are simply astounding. Considering its total mass, we shall probably not go far wrong in assuming that the spectacle of the inky feuds among the foreign Powers imposed a certain caution on the Swiss judgment of world affairs. Thus the power of the pamphlets, which always seeks to do evil, actually did some good in Switzerland. It enabled the Swiss to obtain an unbiassed picture of events abroad, and hence to adopt their own neutral attitude.

The right of asylum, that by-product of neutrality, was exercised in Switzerland from early times, primarily in favour of religious refugees, but later in favour of political exiles also. It is true that other unneutral countries granted asylum to exiles, but that there is a peculiar affinity between neutrality and the right of asylum is shown by the frequency with which the refugee question arises in Swiss history. No country has gone as far as Switzerland in consistently granting asylum to refugees, nor has any proclaimed this Christian behaviour to be also a national duty and felt it to be an expression of gratitude for the unmolested enjoyment of freedom and peace. Thus even Zwingli declared in his " Exhortation to the Godly Confederates " that " all who have been unjustly exiled from other countries have found a refuge in the Confederation . . . For it is clearly to be seen that your freedom is of good not only to yourselves but to the stranger also, that he may find refuge and respite under your protection as in a place of sanctuary."

The sacrifices, the acts of selfless devotion on the part of individual states of the Confederation—and they are countless—have left a track of flame in Swiss history.

Many an episode has passed into poetry, so deep was its humanity, and has been enshrined in the national memory. The refuge given to Arnold of Brescia and Giordano Bruno by Zurich, the rescue of south German leaders in the Peasants' Revolt, the home given to Ulrich von Hutten on the island of Ufenau, the hospitality shown to the French Huguenots, the support of the heroic Waldenses of Piedmont and the Camisards of southern France, the care for English catholics and protestants, not to speak of the protection extended to the countless foreign apostles of liberty, revolutionaries and exiles of all parties in the course of the 19th and 20th centuries—these are familiar matter. A motley host of homeless strangers, outraged and exiled for their religious or political opinions, has found refuge on the saving soil of Switzerland.

The peculiarity of the Swiss right of asylum is that it was granted to all in equal measure. It was extended not only to co-religionists but to religious opponents, not only to men of the same, but to men of other political opinions. Most European nations are represented in the long train of refugees; Germans from every province, Frenchmen, Italians, Englishmen, Hungarians, Spaniards, Poles. The impartiality in the grant of temporary asylum closely links the Swiss right of asylum with the principle of neutrality. This evenhandedness should not be interpreted as indifference ; it should be valued as the result of genuine, morally valuable tolerance. It was an expression of Christian compassion, the faith in love as an effectual power in the community of men.

It is surprising to us today that this far-reaching right of asylum did not apply to fugitive troops. The internment of military persons was unknown in the old Confederation. As the Diet explicitly stated as late as 1673 : " It is unanimously resolved that if fugitives from any army should come, they should be refused admittance, be they who they may." This practise was continued into the 19th century. And the theory of international law was in full agreement with it. On the other hand, under certain conditions Switzerland had the right of allowing troops cut off from the main body to pass straight through the country. The total absence of regulations for internment may be explained by the fear that interned troops might recuperate in Switzerland and undertake a fresh attack on the enemy from that base. Certain remarks by Vattel in his *Droit des Gens*, Vol. III, Par. III, point at any rate in that direction.

Chapter 3

MEANS FOR THE PRESERVATION OF NEUTRALITY

The hope of the old Confederation that, as a result of its abstinence in foreign policy, the whole of its territory should be exempt from war, could only find fulfilment if its neutrality was armed. For the time being, however, the Swiss were incapable of concerted action. The defence of the frontiers was left to the initiative of such individual members of the Confederation as felt themselves in danger. Hence the whole burden fell on the frontier cantons. Whether the others supported them or not was entirely a matter for their own discretion. The question of costs played a determining part here. In the proceedings of the Federal Diet of the time there is an endless succession of appeals for help from the frontier cantons and reluctant consents or evasions on the part of their fellow-members.

Towards the end of the Thirty Years War a real system of defence for the whole Confederation was at last created. The " *Defensional von Wyl* " was concluded in 1644 " for the necessary defence of our common existence and the glorious liberties so dearly bought by our beloved forefathers." The military defence of the frontiers thus became the business of the whole Confederation. A federal war council, with catholic and protestant members on an equal footing, was provided for and put in command of a first army of 12,000 men, to be followed on the approach of danger by a second and a third, so that in the end a total of 36,000 would be available for the defence of the frontiers. This army was made up of contingents from the various cantons which were to be provided on a graded scale. Written military regulations prescribed behaviour both for officers and men which may be described as neutral, although the actual term does not occur. The new federal army law was at once successfully applied against the Swedes and the French. Later on, the mere threat of putting the Defensional into action was enough to keep foreign armies away from the frontiers. When Louis XIV attacked the Franche-Comté for the first time, the cantons revised their Defensional. They extended it to the associates of the Confederation and even gave the war council diplomatic powers, so that it could receive foreign envoys in the same way as the Diet itself.

In the preservation of their neutrality, the Swiss did not only, nor even primarily, take their stand on the military system of the Defensional, but also sought to safeguard their frontiers and frontier districts by treaty agreements. From the beginning of the 16th to the middle of the 18th century the Diet pursued with noteworthy steadfastness the development of a peculiar security device known as the Federal Bastions. In the Confederation it had become almost an article of faith that outlying neutral districts afforded the best protection. A belt of neutralized zones, in which all military action should be prohibited, was to form a protective girdle round the Confederation, otherwise " the body of Helvetia would lie utterly naked and open." It was believed that the Confederation would thus be safeguarded from any severe frontier clashes in the European turmoil. The fact that the shrewdly calculating members of the Diet maintained this protective girdle for centuries, as generations came and went, may be taken as a proof of its effectiveness. In any case, it increased the feeling of security inside the Confederation. Security pacts of this kind were in any case familiar to 17th century thought. We may see in them the birth of international law.

From the time of the Eternal Compact with Hapsburg of 1476, the Austrian towns of Waldshut, Säckingen,

Rheinfelden and Laufenburg had stood under Swiss protection. By prolonged exertions, the Diet succeeded, during the war of the Spanish Succession, in neutralizing these so-called forest cities, as well as the city of Constance and the Fricktal. With that, the Confederation assumed the watch on the Upper Rhine. In this way an actual, if not continuous, system of outworks had been created running from Constance to beyond Basle. Then came the prince-bishopric of Basle, flanking the Confederation on the north-west. The religious alliance between the bishop and the catholic cantons certainly did not suffice to safeguard his territory against invasion, but Berne had included the southern part of the bishopric, from the Münstertal to Bienne, in a perpetual convenant, and thus closed the Jura Gap. From that time on, the southern half of the bishopric had been denoted as an "associate district," a state of things that was respected outside of Switzerland. The northern neutrality belt was bounded on the west by the security zone of Burgundy and the Franche-Comté. It is in connection with these districts that the term "neutrality" makes its first appearance in historical records. As far back as the beginning of the 16th century, the king of France and the princess-regent of the Netherlands had agreed, through the intermediary of the Confederation, to neutralize the French duchy of Burgundy and the Hapsburgian Franche-Comté. The principality of Neuchatel owes its neutrality mainly to the fear of common frontiers with France. By its covenant with certain members of the Confederation, Neuchatel had been bolted into the Confederate bulwarks. At the beginning of the 18th century, the duke of Savoy also offered part of the southern frontier of the Confederation, the long Aosta valley, to the republic of Valais for neutralization, but the project was frustrated by the opposition of France.

In setting up this belt of bastions, the Confederation

was pursuing one of the old maxims of its foreign policy, namely to bound its own territory by a number of small states, independent of each other, and prevent this protective belt from coming under the rule of any one power. The various efforts made for centuries either by the Confederation as a whole or by individual members of it to neutralize their immediate neighbours all sprang from one root—the desire to safeguard the neutrality of the country, if possible in perpetuity. The loose ring of neutral districts created a safeguard of peace which was not based on a system of military fortifications, like the Roman *limes*, but merely on a system of guarantee pacts, though they were destined to prove no more perpetual than any other international covenant. Nevertheless, in the full growth of the *raison d'etat*, of the ruthless application of the power principle, they were, for long periods, recognized as generally binding, as elements in European international law. Not until the epoch of the French Revolution, which was inspired with other ideas, did this system of security grow obsolete. The organization of the Federal Bastions was, from first to last, carried through as a defensive institution. The motive of security, many-facetted and ambiguous as it is, did not, as in France, turn into a pretext for a policy of expansion, but remained faithful to the fundamental idea of neutrality as a demand fully justified from the standpoint both of morality and of international law. The fact that a number of neutralized frontier districts, the bishopric of Basle, the Fricktal, Neuchatel and certain communes in Savoy, were subsequently joined to the Confederation was part of a natural development and provides a justification after the event for the far-sighted exertions of the Diet.

It is further testimony to the Confederation's determination to maintain absolute neutrality that it consistently refused to enter upon international engagements. It rightly feared that such obligations might prove a

c

danger to neutrality and involve the Confederation in foreign disputes. Complete abstention from all guarantees became a principle of its policy. Practically, the Confederation only continued to intervene at all in the affairs of foreign powers for the sake of peace. Warring nations were ceaselessly exhorted to suspend hostilities and begin peace negotiations. In such cases, the Confederation was not even primarily guided by motives of its own interest, although the latter at all times imperatively required peace. The feelings of Christian duty and human compassion were paramount.

In conclusion, it must be admitted that it is impossible to say which of the means of applying the principle of neutrality proved most effective. Such questions often lead to arbitrary answers. One thing, however, is certain ; it was not any one protective measure but the combination of all which promoted the general feeling of security in Switzerland and ensured the success of the policy of neutrality.

Chapter 4

Swiss Neutrality in the Fluctuations of the European Balance of Power during the 18th Century

The 18th century, the period, that is, from the Peace of Utrecht to the outbreak of the French Revolution, is generally regarded as a period of calm in the foreign policy of Switzerland. The great intellectual achievements of a number of outstanding Swiss have cast over the whole epoch a splendour which may easily conjure up a picture of a life of untroubled contemplation. That would, however, be misleading, for the situation of Switzerland both at home and abroad. She certainly managed to keep the peace with her neighbours, but the northern outposts, Basle and Schaffhouse, were fully exposed to the repercussions of the central European wars of succession, and more than once Switzerland felt the covetous eyes of great neighbours fixed upon her. It took all the tried diplomatic skill of the old governments to maintain Swiss territory unaltered amid the ceaseless changes in Europe.

Mercenary service, which had doubled in extent during the first half of the century, was no more prejudicial to Swiss neutrality than it had ever been. On the contrary, foreign observers were at great pains to show that it was an economic necessity. Thus Abraham Stanyan, the diplomatic envoy of England to the protestant cantons, expressed his serious fear that, if Switzerland had to abolish mercenary service, she would again become an independent aggressive power on the continent and thus abandon her neutrality. " If they did not continually drain their country by keeping troops in foreign service, they would soon be so much overstocked in proportion to the extent and fertility of it, that in all probability they would break in upon their neighbours in swarms or go further to seek out new seats." It was agreed both at home and abroad that mercenary service was conducive to neutrality. And indeed in the course of the 18th century, the idea of Swiss neutrality entered deeply into the feeling not only of the Confederation, but of the whole of Europe.

Foreign relations, however, seemed somewhat disturbed after the old alliance with France had expired in 1723, when all efforts to renew it came to grief on the internal dissensions in the Confederation. The situation, however, only became positively threatening at the outbreak of the war of the Polish Succession in 1733. In Savoy and Alsace, French armies advanced against the Hapsburg power of Charles VI, so that war surged against Switzerland both in the south and the north. The most exposed point was the north-west corner of Switzerland. The territory of Basle was pushed wedge-wise between the two main adversaries on the Rhine. Economic pressure could be brought to bear on her by France from the Sundgau and by Austria from the Fricktal. The bases of military pressure were on the one hand the French fort of Huningue, on the other the Austrian garrison at Rhein-felden. This double pressure, trying even in peace time, became intolerable in time of war. Yet the Diet succeeded in commanding respect for the integrity of Swiss territory " by the observance of a total, most strict neutrality towards all the great Powers waging war." The same may be said of the war of the Austrian Succession, 1741–1748, which engaged public opinion in Switzerland far more active and therefore led to more exhaustive discussions of the question of neutrality. This time the protestant cantons even wrote to the " King of Great Britain " urging him to " use his influence in order that the Confederation may enjoy reciprocal and perfect neutrality with the Royal

Hungarian armies." The King replied with the assurance that " he had always had the peace of the Confederation at heart."

In both wars, the principle of economic neutrality was applied with the utmost rigour : " that it should be permitted to any neutral state to supply either side with victuals or any other commodities it had to spare." Further, the creation of a so-called " security zone " three miles wide along the northern frontier of Switzerland, in which all military action should be prohibited, was repeatedly considered. Switzerland hoped for a special safeguarding of her neutrality from a war-free zone of the kind, but the project was abandoned owing to opposition from France.

Abraham Stanyan, in his book *An Account of Switzerland*, published in 1715, a book full of accurate observations and pertinent reflections, remarks that Switzerland only owed her peace to the goodwill of the Powers. But what if that goodwill were to cease ? The experienced statesmen of Switzerland knew only too well that there is no permanence in foreign policy, not even in old, tried friendships. And how little absolute rulers, no matter how high their European standing, respected international treaties was abundantly proved by the behaviour of Frederick the Great towards Austria. It is true that the Seven Years War, 1756–1763, did not encroach on to Swiss territory, so that the Confederation did not even have to man the frontiers. The increased strength of Prussia, and her entry into the concert of the great Powers, shifted the centre of gravity of European politics to the north, and hence seemed to diminish the long pressure on Switzerland. Yet that very intervention of Prussia in world politics meant a new and very grave threat to Swiss peace, namely the union of her two great neighbours, France and Austria. Till that time, Swiss neutrality had literally lived on the rivalry between those two neighbours. In that field of force it had flourished. This traditional element in the European balance of power now vanished, making way for new, unknown and alarming groupings.

By this unexpected union of the two greatest continental Powers, France and Austria, Switzerland found herself hemmed in from Geneva at the south-west tip to the bend in the Rhine at Basle, along the Rhine to the Lake of Constance and up to the Stilfserjoch, and again in the south from Lake Como to Lake Maggiore, so that few links in the chain were lacking. Nothing would have been more comprehensible than that Swiss loyalty should have turned entirely to King Frederick of Prussia in the north. Yet although there was great enthusiasm for his military exploits among the protestant Swiss, they maintained their embargo on the enlistment of mercenaries in Prussian service and avoided loud expressions of sympathy. It was France which provoked a neutrality crisis in 1747 by using a Bernese regiment for the offensive in Germany in contravention of the terms of the capitulation. This incident, however, blew over without causing any great disturbance.

After the peace of exhaustion of Hubertusburg, the diplomatic game went on under cover of stable political conditions. Absolute monarchs of the great Powers looked with special greed at the small states, those relics of the old feudal world. It must never be forgotten that Napoleon's state-exchange had been preceded by a less spectacular, but no less ignoble piece of state-jobbery in the last thirty years of the 18th century. The news of the first partition of Poland was a dreadful warning to the Confederate republic whose name had so often been coupled with Poland's, though the differences between them were greater than the likenesses. There was an almost general distrust of Switzerland's eastern neighbour and hereditary arch-enemy Austria. From the young, active and ambitious Joseph of Hapsburg the worst might be expected. He was generally believed to have been the prime mover against Poland.

It is a fact that plans for a possible amputation of Switzerland had been discussed in the cabinets of the great Powers. How seriously they were taken is not the point at issue here. It is, however, certain that Switzerland knew of the discussions and was in a state of great anxiety. For the Confederation, of necessity, responded to every quiver of the European balance. It was in the powerful allied fronts that the Swiss began to see their most effective protection against Austrian irredentism. Besides, since France had lost her predominance with the rise of Prussia, her superiority no longer seemed so absolute as to make a Swiss alliance turn into dependence.

One measure of Vergenne's new French foreign policy had consisted in grouping the minor states round France in order to restore her prestige with respect to the rising great Powers. One factor in this system was an alliance between France and Switzerland, not merely for the regulation of their common interests, but as an element in a great European order. The fear of Austria led Switzerland to close with Vergenne's offer, and the French alliance was renewed with great pomp in 1777. Clause VI contained something like a declaration of the principle of neutrality. " . . . *et comme le présent traité absolument défensif ne doit préjudicier ni déroger en rien à la neutralité des parties, les louables cantons et leurs alliés déclarent ici de la manière la plus expresse de vouloir l'observer et maintenir dans tous les cas et sans distinction vis-à-vis de toutes les puissances.*" By their French alliance the various members of the Confederation had once more acted in concert as a single federal state towards a foreign country and made a solemn declaration of their neutrality.

Chapter 5

ATTACKS ON SWISS NEUTRALITY
BY REVOLUTIONARY FRANCE

At the outbreak of the French Revolution, the question of neutrality did not stand in the foreground of Swiss policy. It was not until the revolutionary armies had swept over the French frontier and come into conflict with Europe, that is, after the beginning of the revolutionary wars in the spring of 1792, that the question of neutrality became a practical issue for Switzerland. Of course, even then there could be no question of neutrality of feeling. The local governments, and with them the classes from which they were drawn, that is, the politically, socially and economically prominent families, further, privileged members of the bourgeoisie and even the professional officers in foreign armies—all these stood by old, royalist France. In the Confederation the friends of the Revolution formed only a small minority, mainly recruited from the younger progressives in the cantonal capitals and country towns.

Meanwhile the Diet was responsible for the neutrality of the Confederation. There were in particular two things which embarrassed relations between France and Switzerland at this time, firstly the revolutionary propaganda which poured over Switzerland from its fountain-head in Paris, and against which the French parts of Switzerland were by no means immune, secondly the emigration from France. The French émigrés settled mainly in the frontier cities of Soleure, Fribourg and Neuchatel, and waited for the day of their return. The French government could not but regard their presence as a danger.

Yet in spite of these elements of discord between Switzerland and her old ally, the Diet pronounced its declaration of neutrality in the form which had by that time become customary. It is certain that the great majority of the people approved of this decision. It was communicated to the belligerent Powers and to the commanders of armies operating in the neighbourhood of the Swiss frontiers. The Diet sent 1,300 men to the threatened frontier at Basle, and unanimously resolved to extend the neutrality of the Confederation to the principality of Neuchatel, the prince-bishopric of Basle and the city of Geneva, thus strengthening the defences of the western frontier and thereby making good a long-standing sin of omission.

This official neutrality remained in force even when the relations between France and Switzerland were subjected to one of the severest strains they ever had to undergo. On August 7, the Paris mob, in storming the Tuileries, murdered the Swiss Guard as the defenders of the throne. Further, the French government illegally dismissed the Swiss mercenaries stationed all over the country and sent them home without pay. The feeling of wounded pride would have been the best means of driving the Confederation into the arms of the Coalition, nor did the Allied diplomats fail to use all their persuasive powers to that end. But yet again the sober, realistic spirit of the Swiss statesmen gained the upper hand. The Diet of September, 1792, repeated its declaration of neutrality.

France herself had strictly respected Swiss neutrality at the beginning of her war against the Coalition. When General Custine marched into the bishopric of Basle he occupied only that part of the country which indubitably belonged to the German Empire and in which there were German troops, namely the district of Porrentruy. At that time the French Revolution was advancing victoriously all over Europe. We may well ask why, in this, the first flush of its power, revolutionary France did not overrun the Confederation too. The reason was that Swiss neutrality was of capital importance to her, especially from the economic standpoint. The Allied blockade formed a ring round France which was open only along the Swiss frontier. Since France was not economically self-supporting, she sought to obtain what she lacked in Switzerland. For a number of years the French Revolution was actually dependent on transit through Switzerland for necessary supplies.

Under the lasting impression of these political and economic events, there was a thorough clarification of Swiss opinion, which split into two opposing camps. Governments and people divided into a war party and a neutrality party. The former was led by N. F. de Steiger, the chief magistrate of Berne. From the outset he proclaimed his firm conviction that Switzerland must abandon her traditional neutrality and join the European crusade against the French Revolution, not for reasons of self-preservation, but as a moral duty. The neutrality party found support mainly at Zurich and Basle. Under the powerful influence of Zurich, then the *Vorort* or official representative of the Confederation, the whole of eastern Switzerland joined it. Its aim was to maintain the traditional neutrality whatever happened, even at the cost of further and humiliating concessions to the abounding military strength of its neighbour. The war about the correct interpretation of neutrality was waged in pamphlets.

The new rulers in Paris were chiefly aggrieved by the fact that the Steiger party was protecting the doings of the English minister. As time went on, it became increasingly clear that England was the great adversary of the French Revolution. The conservative, insular power pitted itself against the revolutionary, continental one and struggled with its century-old rival for the seas, the continents, the mastery of the world. Since Pitt could not get the upper hand of the French armies on the Continent, he attempted to set a counter-revolution going in France by supporting the existing and growing royalist party. Projects of this kind could most easily be worked from Switzerland. In William Wickham, Pitt found a diplomat who was fully conversant with conditions on the Continent and in Switzerland, and whose energy, ingenuity and astuteness marked him out to take charge of this onerous task. Swiss territory, moreover, was an excellent coign of vantage and the best base for a secret service extending all over the Continent. Wickham worked with the royalist agency in Paris, bribed disaffected generals, introduced counter-revolutionary literature into France, and accumulated war material along the Jura frontier, the point at which the inner and outer counter-revolutionary movements came into contact. Berne's toleration of Wickham's underground and unneutral activities was compromising for the whole of Switzerland, and it can only be explained by the sympathy of the Steiger party for England's cause.

The French Directoire was determined to suffer Wickham's activities no longer, and even to respect Swiss neutrality only as long as it worked to the advantage of France. As the armies of the Directoire gained victory after victory in the south of Germany and the north of Italy, and Switzerland was almost entirely encircled, the Directoire increased its demands in proportion. In the end it demanded Wickham's expulsion, a grave infringement of Swiss neutrality. In order to spare the Swiss government still greater embarrassments, Wickham left the country of his own accord. It was on the southern frontier of Switzerland, however, that France dealt most unceremoniously with Swiss neutrality. Since Napoleon had conquered Upper Italy, and was sole master there,

there was no end to the violations of the transalpine
territories and of plans of attack on the integrity of Swiss
territory. Finally, on October 10, 1797, Napoleon decreed
that it was open to the three provinces of Valtellina,
Chiavenna and Bormio, till then part of the Grisons, to
join the Cisalpine Republic. The loss of the three valleys
meant a painful breach in the strategic power of Switzerland and hence a danger to her neutrality.

Behind these repeated French onslaughts, it was easy
to discern the determination of the new Directoire to
disregard the neutrality of Switzerland should occasion
arise. There were large circles in Switzerland which sat
waiting with folded arms, as men wait for an impending
natural catastrophe. A few, however, whether from
wounded pride or wounded vanity, egged on the French
to armed intervention, and even gave them hints as to how
that intervention could be justified by history and
precedent.

The Bernese Colonel Weiss attempted to dissuade the
French from invading Switzerland by a pamphlet :
" *Réveillez-vous, Suisses, le danger approache,*" on the
grounds that Swiss neutrality was in the interests of
France and that its violation would be the signal for long
and ruinous wars. It was, of course, in vain. In 1798 the
French advanced into Switzerland, the great struggle for
the passes in the heart of Europe began, Suvoroff crossed
the Alps and Europe saw what a destruction of Swiss
neutrality meant.

Chapter 6

FICTITIOUS NEUTRALITY AT THE TIME
OF THE HELVETIC REPUBLIC
AND THE MEDIATION

After France had revolutionized Switzerland, the French Directoire, with the object of tightening up its relations with the Helvetic Republic, wished to renew the alliance. Since the beginning of the 16th century, the Confederation had been in defensive alliance with the French monarchy. This secured enough freedom of movement for Switzerland to prevent her having to take part in the French war policy. The French Directoire, however, now demanded that Switzerland should enter into an offensive alliance with it, by which she would have been harnessed to the war policy of the imperial revolution. In spite of violent resistance on the part of the Helvetic Directory, it was eventually forced by French threats to sign the treaty dictated by Paris. This treaty provided for mutual military assistance, obliged the Helvetic Republic to keep the roads open to France for military and commercial purposes, and deprived Switzerland of her right of asylum. The whole was tantamount to a surrender of Swiss neutrality.

The danger dreaded by the opponents of the offensive alliance did not fail to appear immediately afterwards at the outbreak of the second Coalition war. According to the terms of the alliance, Switzerland had to provide 18,000 men for auxiliary brigades in French pay and 20,000 militiamen on her own account. Since the main opposing armies had taken up their positions in the south of Germany and Upper Italy, Switzerland, with her Alpine passes, occupied an important key position. She now became the European theatre of war on an unprecedented scale. The foreign hordes left behind them a devastated country and an utterly exhausted people. Plunder, rapine, quarterings and forced supplies swelled the havoc immeasurably.

In its disillusionment, the people began to accuse the government of having brought these terrible sufferings on Switzerland by their surrender of her neutrality. In various parts of the country there were armed risings. But when the Diet entered into negotiations even with England, Austria and Russia, Napoleon intervened with lightning speed. He issued a proclamation imposing his mediation on Switzerland and ordered the disbandment of the Swiss forces. When England reminded him of Switzerland's right of self-determination and the Diet took up an attitude of passive resistance, he occupied the country.

Thus as far as Swiss neutrality was concerned, the epoch of the Mediation set in under anything but favourable auspices. How Napoleon imagined the future relations of Switzerland to France can be seen in his own words : " I shall never suffer any influence in Switzerland but my own, even though it should cost me 100,000 men." Napoleon had drafted the Acts of Mediation with an eye to his own requirements. They were to keep Switzerland weak and in permanent dependence on France. He forced her to conclude a military capitulation by which the best part of the Swiss forces came into his hands. Swiss neutrality was rendered entirely a fiction by the fact that Napoleon deprived Swiss foreign policy of its freedom. He only allowed her to conclude further capitulations with powers friendly to himself. That was a blow aimed at Napoleon's chief enemy, England, whose Swiss mercenaries had just reached their greatest strength. Switzerland soon found herself surrounded by Napoleon's empire and satellite states. There was no further possibility of an independent foreign policy, for instance a connection with unconquerable England.

That Napoleon, even at the climax of his power, could turn Swiss neutrality to good use, was shown by his war against Austria in 1805. The neutrality of Swiss territory was not violated by the belligerents during that war, while Prussia, who had declared herself neutral, had to suffer the transit of French and Russian troops. On this occasion Napoleon saw his advantage, not in marching through Swiss territory, but in shielding France against Austrian attacks by the armed neutrality of Switzerland.

The best interpretation of Swiss neutrality at the time of Napoleon's domination was given by Napoleon himself in the war against Austria in 1809. As always, the Diet had again issued a proclamation of neutrality and ordered the frontiers to be manned. In order to obtain from France an explicit recognition of Swiss neutrality, Landammann Reinhard hurried to Regensburg, where that famous conversation took place in which the Emperor candidly expressed his own idea of it : "*Vis-à-vis de moi, cette neutralité est un mot vide de sens qui ne vous sert qu'autant que je le veux.*"

Napoleon also gravely threatened Swiss independence and neutrality by territorial cessions. In 1806 he bartered the principality of Neuchatel to the king of Prussia for Hanover and parts of southern Germany. What the vigilant Confederation of the early 18th century had forestalled now happened. French troops were able to advance without let or hindrance over the Jura into the neighbourhood of Berne. Following up the seizure of the Vatican state and the North Sea coasts, Napoleon also put an end to the fictitious independence of the Valais by annexing it to France in 1810. In the same year, by a brutal act of violence and without any warning, he had the canton of Ticino and Misox in the Grisons occupied by Italian troops.

Nor did Napoleon grant any neutrality to the economic life of Switzerland. The Confederation began to feel how utterly it was at the mercy of France when the increase on the duty on cotton, which was aimed at England, was also applied to itself. Napoleon called on Switzerland to close her frontiers to English imports. Intimidated by French mass confiscations, the Diet voluntarily submitted to the blockade. Thus outraged, the economy of Switzerland suffered appalling distress under the continental blockade.

The Diet, after the decisive battle of Leipzig, declared on November 18 that " it would take up a perfectly neutral attitude in the present wars, and would maintain that neutrality impartially towards all the great belligerent Powers." In spite of statements to the contrary in a few Swiss newspapers, it may be confidently asserted that there was no difference of opinion in the Diet on the principle of neutrality. It was more difficult to come to any general agreement as to how that neutrality was to be defended. The Diet certainly declared itself independent of the continental system, which was tantamount to a step towards the resumption of neutrality, but it could not bring itself to recall the regiments in French service. Its military preparations were also inadequate. The scantiness of the levy actually cast suspicion on Swiss neutrality in the eyes of the Allies.

Chapter 7

THE BREACH OF NEUTRALITY IN 1813

It was in Germany, quite especially, that the declaration of neutrality by the Diet provoked the bitterest disappointment. Had these neutral Swiss, people wondered, no spark of the spirit of the old *Eidgenossen,* those old Germanic heroes who had been held up as an inspiration to the troops at Leipzig? The saga of the liberation of Switzerland had swelled to romantic proportions, and present events had been so directly interpreted in its light, that in the end Tell appeared as the guardian angel of the German armies. In the German mind, the boundaries between the Swiss and the German nations began to fade. It was taken for granted that the brothers of the Confederation would lend their active support.

With hopes raised so high, it is not surprising that, immediately after the battle of Leipzig, the question of Swiss neutrality took the forefront in German political writing. In all the literature dealing with the Confederation, from the letter and newspaper article to the work of historical research, dissatisfaction with the manifesto of neutrality was openly expressed. The gravamen of the charge against the Swiss was the mercenary capitulations. While the contemporary doctrine of international law declared the supply of mercenary troops to be compatible with neutrality, German publications on international law after 1813 would only concede to the Swiss procedure the name of partial neutrality. German journalism went still farther. Mainly on moral grounds they launched an embittered attack on the maintenance of Swiss neutrality. To the Germans, who conceived that they were fighting for the supreme ideals of European humanity, Swiss neutrality looked like a betrayal of timeless, indestructible

D

values, and even as a sin against nature, since it ran counter to the idea of the German nation. The ultimate conclusions drawn from this idea of a Germanic race culminated in the demand that Switzerland should be united with Germany.

These ideas did not only haunt the minds of a few writers. It has been proved that even prominent statesmen seriously discussed plans of the kind. But all intentions and aims directed to that end were thwarted by the opposition first of Metternich and later of Talleyrand, whose legitimist conservatism was the dominant force in the world of real politics of the day. The former aimed at replacing the previous French ascendancy in Europe by that of Austria, but not of Germany as a whole.

A survey of the diplomatic correspondence of the time shows perfectly unambiguously that Metternich was aiming at a violation of Swiss neutrality for political and military reasons and was using the most subtle methods of his diplomatic art to that end. Investigation further shows that Czar Alexander and Emperor Francis at first vigorously opposed the plan. The well-intentioned king of Prussia, however, declared to the Swiss embassy which presented the declaration of neutrality to the headquarters of the Allies : " Neutrality is a word which has fallen into complete discredit. I have myself learned how difficult it is to maintain in practice, and as far as I am personally concerned, I never could be convinced of its utility. I rather believe that it would be to the real advantage of the Swiss to make common cause with us." And Metternich actually encouraged Switzerland to take an active part in the war.

The Swiss government, however, did not fall in with the Chancellor's suggestion. He then found support in an unexpected quarter. He received from the secret agents he had sent to Switzerland a report of a conversation with General von Wattenwyl. All that Wattenwyl wanted was to come to an agreement as to the forms to be observed so that his own responsibility might be covered. With this report in hand, Metternich was able to persuade his emperor to allow the general staff to take the preliminary steps for the occupation of Switzerland. The Allied monarchs believed in good faith that they were acting in agreement with the military command of the Confederation.

In reply to an Allied ultimatum, Swiss headquarters forthwith issued the order for withdrawal. The commandant of the Basle district further concluded an agreement by which the Allies promised the Confederation the unmolested withdrawal of all Swiss troops on the Rhine with military honours, with arms and baggage, with artillery and munitions, and also engaged to safeguard Basle as far as possible from attack from the French side. It is obvious from all these arrangements that the General regarded the defensive power of the Swiss army as inadequate. Between Schaffhouse and Basle, some fifteen battalions numbering hardly 8,000 men with a handful of artillery were scattered along the frontier. The whole was little more than a military demonstration in face of an invading army of 200,000 men.

The passivity with which the breach of the promised neutrality was accepted was a precedent which weighed heavily on succeeding generations. We may well ask whether a few shots fired from the Swiss bank of the Rhine would not have brought Metternich's whole plan to grief. Both the Czar and the Austrian Emperor wished to enter Switzerland only as her friends and allies. In any case armed defence has always imposed respect on the enemy and had its effect on future events.

The responsibility for the lamentable failure of Switzerland to rise to the occasion rests, in varying degrees, with her leaders. The Landammann and the General must be acquitted of treachery. The Confederation succumbed to overpowering pressure from the outside and to disruptive forces inside the country, to the lack of the spirit of self-sacrifice in a people worn out by long foreign domination and to the jealousy and incompetence of its political and military leaders.

On December 21, 1813, the day on which the Allies entered Basle, they handed over to the Landammann a written statement giving their reasons for the violation of Swiss neutrality. They recognized Switzerland's right to absolute sovereignty. It had been suppressed by Napoleon, but by him only, and, like that of other European states, would soon be restored. The Allies further gave their solemn promise not to lay down arms until they had obtained for Switzerland the restitution of the territories forcibly annexed by France. Thus at the very moment at which the Allies committed their violation of Swiss neutrality, they formally engaged to restore it as soon as Switzerland was free of foreign influence.

For the time being, however, the Allies paid no heed whatever to the fulfilment of their promises. They marched straight through the Swiss midlands, passed Berne, Soleure, Neuchatel and Fribourg and quitted Swiss territory at Geneva. Lateral columns had already turned aside over the Jura into France. Once again, as in 1799, Switzerland was full of foreign soldiéry ; even if the country did not, as then, serve as the theatre of war, it suffered terribly from the perpetual presence of large armies. The passage of the main body was followed, till the end of the war, by reinforcements of all kinds. The quartering of huge masses of troops on the population was a heavy burden, for they had to be not only quartered, but fed too. The greatest sufferings, however, were due to the contagious diseases brought into the country. In many places military hospitals had to be set up, and typhoid and typhus spread to the population.

The first result of the transit of the Allies was the collapse of the Mediation. Before anarchy could gain ground in Switzerland, a Confederate assembly met. It abrogated the Acts of Mediation as being of French origin and guaranteed freedom to the former subject districts. A further result was the recovery of the territories lost to France. With that, the Allies fulfilled one of the promises given in their statement and often repeated since. For that matter their loudly proclaimed principles were by no means at variance with their own interests. It was their object to strengthen all the small countries between France and Central Europe, and to use them as buffer-states should France again take the offensive. For that reason they united Belgium with Holland and Genoa with Sardinia, and it was for the same motives that the territory of Switzerland was rounded off. She was allowed to admit Neuchatel, Geneva and the Valais into the Confederation. The incorporation of these three cantons fulfilled at any rate one of the conditions necessary for the restoration of absolute neutrality. The Swiss frontiers were improved, that is, they were made easier to defend.

Chapter 8

RECOGNITION OF THE PERMANENT NEUTRALITY
OF SWITZERLAND

The Swiss delegation to the Congress of Vienna was,
unfortunately, composed of members both of the old and
the new Switzerland who stood in each others' way and
thus prevented any united action or forcible argument.
Multifarious as the points on the Swiss programme were,
they were almost exclusively concerned with the
rectification of the frontiers and the establishment of the
cantonal constitutions. At one point, however, all
dissention, all intercantonal disputes were silenced—
namely, the question of neutrality. In the instructions
issued to the Swiss delegation, stringent orders were
given respecting the neutrality of the Confederation, and
here all were united in a common cause. The instructions
enlarged with unwonted emphasis on the question of
neutrality. It is called " from of old the mainstay of
Swiss policy." The whole of Europe, the instructions
state, sees in the neutrality and peace of Switzerland a
pledge of its own security and one of the cardinal conditions of the political balance which had now to be
restored.

The first step of the Congress was to hand the Swiss
question over to a special committee of the Quadruple
Alliance. This committee on Switzerland, composed of
prominent and famous statesmen, dealt in the first place
only with the rectification of the frontiers and internal
territorial changes in Switzerland. In its final report, the
committee stated that the continued existence and
sovereignty of the nineteen cantons were the foundation
on which the political system of Switzerland rested.
Thereupon, on March 20, 1815, the eight Congress

Powers issued a statement to the effect that the perpetual neutrality of Switzerland within her new frontiers should be recognized and guaranteed on condition that the Diet gave its consent to the stipulations contained in the statement. In this document, the term " *neutralité perpétuelle* " is used for the first time. This expression was therefore not introduced into international law by Switzerland, but by other powers. The Diet accepted the conditions laid down by the Powers and expressed its thanks for the promise " *de reconnaître et de garantir la neutralité perpétuelle que l'intérêt général de l'Europe réclame en faveur du corps helvétique.*"

The discussions of the fate of Switzerland having been unduly protracted, they were thus brought to a surprisingly speedy conclusion. The reason was the sudden return of Napoleon from Elba. Napoleon's landing in the south of France and his triumphal march to Paris also created unanimity among the Swiss delegates. In view of the growing danger in the west, the Diet ordered the Federal force of 30,000 men to be kept under arms. And now the great question was what course the Confederation would pursue in the general struggle against Napoleon. The Congress Powers, Great Britain, Prussia, Austria and Russia, had, of course, renewed their old alliances and engaged to send 150,000 men each against " the Gallic beast of prey." Napoleon, however, now gave his solemn assurance that he had no further intention of disturbing the peace of Europe and that he would absolutely respect the sovereignty of other states. In view of this, the Swiss democrats, and quite particularly the cantons which had formerly been subject districts and had gained their freedom through the revolution, actively advocated the maintenance of neutrality. What Stratford Canning wrote to Castlereagh was no more than the truth : " The main bias of the population is to neutrality." Although a few aristocrats preached the cause of union with the Coalition, Switzerland would not, of her own free will, have left the path of strict neutrality. To make her do so, it took exceedingly strong political pressure from outside.

While even in 1813 the Allies were still vacillating on the subject of Swiss neutrality, they now never even thought of respecting it. In calling upon Switzerland to join the Coalition, what they meant was that Switzerland should temporarily abandon her strict neutrality in order to safeguard her perpetual neutrality for the future. They promised to respect the principle of neutrality, and Switzerland was only required to provide for a reliable defence of her frontiers in order to cover her own operations. The great Powers were not, of course, primarily concerned with obtaining the support of the small Swiss state. What they wanted was transit through Switzerland. It was only after grave misgivings on the Swiss side had been overcome that a convention was arrived at. This agreement was a strange compromise between the maintenance of the traditional neutrality of Switzerland and her union with the Allies.

The point which most gravely compromises Swiss neutrality stands in Article VI, which certainly abandons the claim to the use of military roads on principle, but adds, as an exception : " If, in case of emergency, the common interest should require the immediate passage of Allied troops through any part of the territory of the Confederation, the consent of the Diet will be sought." Thus the form of neutrality was preserved ; in substance it was abandoned. For nobody imagined that, if the Allies should claim the right of passage, the Diet would have any other course but to submit.

The Diet issued a proclamation informing the Swiss forces of the union with the Allies, and gave orders that the Allied troops were to be treated as friends and brothers in arms. Shortly afterwards news arrived of the battle of Waterloo and Napoleon's abdication. The Confederation could now have demobilized the army, but suddenly Basle was quite unexpectedly bombarded for an hour from the fortress of Huningue. General Bachmann collected his troops and prepared to avenge the attack. He 'was, however, coolly ordered by the Diet to hold the Defensional in holy respect. A few trifling attacks on Swiss frontier patrols, however, succeeded in rousing the Diet. It resolved by a majority to give the General plenary powers to occupy a post on French territory. He crossed the frontier with 22,000 men, helped to force Fort Blamont to capitulate, occupied the valley of the Doubs as far as Morteau and ordered the garrison of Basle to take part in the siege of Huningue with guns and men.

The Diet seems always to have had qualms about this escapade in the offensive. How right it was in curbing the old General's zeal is made startlingly clear by a number of mutinies which followed. Some contingents refused to march on the grounds that they could only be used for the defence of their native soil. Such incidents go to prove how unpopular the Burgundian campaign was with large sections of the Swiss public.

After the return of Louis XVIII to his capital, there was no sense in continuing the Swiss operations in France. General Bachmann, who felt himself to be under old obligations to the Bourbons, began to withdraw with his troops. Though we may believe that Switzerland could not have acted otherwise than she did under foreign pressure, it is regrettable that she should have abandoned her defensive attitude, if only for a short time. This transgression against the hereditary principle of neutrality, however, had no practical results, unless we can regard the dismantling of the fort of Huningue as a success of the policy, meagre though it was in comparison with the sacrifices it cost.

Since Switzerland had accepted the conditions laid down in the Declaration of Vienna of March 20, 1815, she hoped that the recognition of Swiss neutrality would now find official expression. The Powers, however, turned a deaf ear to the repeated petitions of the Diet, and dragged out the final drafting of the acts of recognition until Napoleon's empire of the Hundred Days had collapsed. After her contribution to the Napoleonic wars, during the negotiations for the second Peace of Paris, Switzerland tried at last to reach her goal. An extremely adroit and very reliable diplomat, Pictet de Rougement, was sent to Paris to represent Switzerland with the five Powers. The first item of his instructions was to request that the solemn act of recognition of the perpetual neutrality of Switzerland should, according to promise, be drafted.

But again, as at Vienna, it was not neutrality which was the main point of negotiation with Switzerland, but the rectification of the frontiers. In order to secure direct communication by land with Switzerland for his native city of Geneva, Pictet insisted quite particularly on the cession of Versoix, which he obtained. He also succeeded in acquiring from Sardinia the communes which were indispensable if Geneva were to be released from her enclave. As a condition of the cession, Savoy demanded that the Savoyard provinces of Chablais and Faucigny, and the whole territory in the north of Ugine should participate in Swiss neutrality. The great significance of this neutralization of the north of Savoy, a peculiar creation of modern international law, was that Switzerland paid that price for the rounding-off of the territory of Geneva.

A general survey of the external configuration of Switzerland in 1815 as compared with that of the old Confederation of 1798 shows how much more favourable were the frontiers Switzerland had acquired in the interim.

The territory of Basle, which had once jutted out to the north-west between the Austrian Fricktal and the French Sundgau, and hence offered perpetual occasion for the violation of neutrality by the transit of troops, had considerably improved its exposed position. On the eastern side Switzerland had acquired the Fricktal and was not required to restore to a victorious Austria the gift Napoleon had made her. In the west, Basle was now covered, in part at any rate, by territory of the Bishopric of Basle which also fell to Switzerland's portion. Finally, the extremely exposed south-west tip of Switzerland, Geneva, was now in direct communication with the Confederation. The way had been prepared for all these frontier rectifications by the old Confederate system of the Federal Bastions. The districts now acquired had all, at some time or other, been included in Swiss neutrality. Their permanent union with Switzerland is thus seen to be the organic product of a long history and thus finds its inward justification. It was not the result of arbitrary diplomatic action, like so many of the frontier rectifications of Napoleonic and post-Napoleonic manipulations.

Though Switzerland could not carry through her territorial aims in Paris, she was entirely successful in establishing her claim to neutrality. Originally it was the English Minister in Switzerland, Stratford Canning, who had been charged with the drafting of the acts of neutrality. Since he did nothing in the two months allowed him, Castlereagh and Capo d'Istria requested Pictet de Rougemont, the Swiss plenipotentiary in Paris, to draft the act himself. It was an unprecedented stroke of good fortune that the declaration of neutrality which was to be formally promulgated by the Powers should have been drawn up by a Swiss, for it thus became possible to avoid in the very wording of the act anything that might have been prejudicial to Swiss interests.

Pictet's draft was amended only on trifling points. On November 20th, the declaration was signed by the five great Powers, Austria, France, Great Britain, Prussia and Russia, and subsequently by Portugal. What a relief this meant to the statesmen of Switzerland may well be imagined. After a period of continual breaches of neutrality lasting for nearly twenty years, breaches which were at times tantamount to its abandonment, the old maxim of Swiss foreign policy was revived, clarified and strengthened by its recognition in international law.

The declaration of neutrality, the original text of which is reproduced in the Appendix, begins with a survey of the circumstances in which it took shape. The body of the act then contains a declaration of great importance in international law, namely that the Powers "*font par le présent Acte une reconnaissance formelle et authentique de la neutralité perpétuelle de la Suisse, et Elles lui garantissent l'intégrité et l'inviolablité de son territoire dans ses nouvelles limites, telles qu'elles sont fixées tant par L'Acte du Congrès de Vienne que par le Traité de Paris de ce jour et telles qu'elles le seront ultérieurement.*"

For centuries the Confederation had maintained this principle in its foreign affairs, more or less absolutely, but always in a way consistent with the contemporary provisions of international law, and sometimes even in advance of it. The recognition of neutrality by the Powers meant that the state of neutrality hitherto based on custom was now based on international law. This must not be taken to mean that the Powers created the neutrality of Switzerland as they did that of Belgium, for instance, in 1831 and 1839. There was no question of recognition there. The Powers declared Belgium, federated with Holland since the Congress of Vienna, an independent state and guaranteed its neutrality at the same time. Belgium's neutrality was distinct from that of Switzerland in that it had never been a traditional political principle of the country ; on the contrary, in the European conflicts Belgium had taken her share as a part now of one great power, now of another. Her permanent neutrality was created by a voluntary act and dictated to the Belgian state. Belgium was explicitly instructed to observe towards all states the neutrality she had reluctantly accepted, while Switzerland, on the contrary, urgently besought the Powers to recognize at last, in all due form, her century-old principle.

The explicit guarantee refers to the integrity of Swiss territory ; its object is to protect that territory from attack by other states. Should Swiss territory be violated —that is the meaning of the guarantee—the guarantors commit themselves to restoring its integrity, for territorial integrity is of the substance of neutrality. Thus a territorial guarantee expands into a guarantee of neutrality.

Switzerland has at all times deduced from the guarantee of her neutrality a claim for help against its violators. Nor has that claim ever been seriously contested. The only question which remained unsettled was whether the Powers could infer a right to independent intervention from the guarantee they had assumed. This reading was decisively rejected by the Federal Council in 1917. England and the United States wished to attach conditions to the recognition of Swiss neutrality. In its answer the Council established its principle : " The Confederation claims the sole right of deciding whether and under what conditions it will recognize the necessity of calling in the assistance of foreign Powers." Thus Switzerland conceded to the guarantors no right to take measures for the protection of Swiss neutrality without the consent of Switzerland, still more against her will.

From the outset, Switzerland consistently upheld the view that the Powers could not infer from the assumption of the guarantee a right to enquire whether the neutrality they had promised to protect was really being maintained by her. To admit such a right would be tantamount to a control of Switzerland by the Powers and to offering the guarantors occasion for permanent interference in the home affairs of the Confederation.

One of the most important provisions of the Acts of Neutrality is that not only the neutrality, but also the integrity and sovereignty of Switzerland are in the true interests of Europe. The implications of this passage can only be understood by a reference to the historical background. For many years Switzerland had been subjected to an excessive French influence which had amounted to an abolition of her neutrality. On December 21st, 1813, the Allies had declared that complete freedom from foreign influence was the first condition of the existence and recognition of true neutrality. After the victory over Napoleon, however, Metternich obstinately endeavoured to replace the former French influence on Switzerland by that of Austria. For Switzerland, that would have meant exchanging the French for an Austrian protectorate. Pictet, in order to forestall any development of the kind, which he feared, in order, indeed, to prevent any future interference, introduced the above provision into his draft, and it was against Metternich's will that it was accepted.

Even though the clause can only be understood on its historical background, its importance is general and not only applicable to circumstances prevailing at the time of the Congress of Vienna. It is of its nature a statement of a fact of political experience which finds its confirmation in the history of three hundred years of Swiss neutrality. Long experience in the past was conceived to hold good for the future ; a violation of Swiss neutrality would turn out to be prejudicial to the whole of the European world of states. The insight into the European necessity of the principle of Swiss neutrality gives Switzerland far greater

security than any, even the most solemn, guarantees.
This is especially true of periods in which international
law, that is, the sanctity of international treaties, is somewhat at a discount.

Chapter 9

LIMITATION OF NEUTRALITY UNDER THE CONTROL OF THE
GREAT POWERS

With the promulgation of the Acts of Neutrality,
Switzerland had laid down her programme of foreign
policy. That the rulers of the Confederation had fully
grasped the aims of Swiss foreign policy can be seen in the
President's speech at the opening of the Diet in 1816.
Any possible protectorate on the part of the great Powers
was then finally repudiated, a step which seemed the more
necessary in that Switzerland had been confronted with
the great question of whether she was going to join the
great international security treaty of the Holy Alliance.
It is highly characteristic that the objections to joining it
were loudest in England and Switzerland. In both countries
it ran counter to tradition to join a union embracing the
whole of Europe, and hence to bind foreign policy for an
indefinite period. Great Britain avoided such engagements because they seemed to encroach on its traditional
policy of splendid isolation, Switzerland because she
feared it would imply acceptance of far-reaching commitments and hence a limitation of her traditional neutrality.
It was only when Switzerland had received the assurance
that she could make a reservation in favour of her
neutrality that, in 1817, she declared her readiness to
join in extremely cautious and reserved terms. For the
statesmen of Switzerland had no intention of yielding up,
for a mess of pottage, the jewel of neutrality so lately won.
They were not going to barter their absolute for a
differential neutrality.

The fears that Switzerland, as a member of the Holy
Alliance, would be committed to giving military assistance
and hence become involved in international strife

proved groundless. The explicit assumption, however, that the Holy Alliance might lead to intervention in Swiss affairs proved more than right. In 1815, the chorus of the Great Powers was singing in such perfect unison that Switzerland was not allowed to strike a note of her own. Resistance to the solid front of the Powers was as fruitless as it had been to Napoleon's European supremacy. As the great Powers each assumed, in increasing measure, a definite political constitution and a definite political mentality, it became the more difficult for Switzerland to abide by her old and peculiar political outlook and her independent foreign policy. It was only when England began to withdraw from the Holy Alliance, taking France with her, only when Europe began to split into a western and an eastern bloc, that Swiss neutrality could develop more freely.

Among the neighbour states of the Swiss Confederation, it was Austria which loomed largest, for it was the leading statesman of Austria who was also the conductor of the European chorus. In his European system, Metternich had assigned a perfectly definite part to neutral Switzerland. She was to be an armed factor in shielding Austria against further attack by French imperialism, and, in her position as a buffer-state, was to act as a shock-absorber. Beyond that, however, the Confederation was to be interposed between the south of Germany and Austria and the tide of revolutionary ideas rising in the centres of unrest in France and Italy, and thus help to immunize central Europe against the bacillus of revolution. From this European obligation, Metternich inferred the right of the great Powers to intervene in Switzerland should the individual cantons show too little energy in action against the international conspiracy of revolution. Switzerland had her responsibility towards Europe. The Austrian Chancellor actually made his recognition of Swiss neutrality dependent on the adoption of a particular

E

attitude by the Confederation. Thereby his interpretation of the treaties of 1815 became quite untenable. For the great Powers, by their declaration of neutrality, had recognized Swiss neutrality without attaching conditions to it.

France was now following the lead of Austria in her European policy, though in Switzerland she took up a peculiarly French standpoint. To her regret, there could be no further question of resuming the alliance to its former extent. That would have been contrary to the neutrality of Switzerland, which had been internationally recognized in the meantime. France therefore contented herself with entering upon military capitulations with Switzerland. The storming of the Tuileries had taught the Bourbons what a treasure of loyalty they possessed in the Swiss Guards. While the eastern Powers had only lately declared a conclusion of mercenary agreements with France alone to be unneutral, they now saw in the same act nothing which could be regarded as prejudicial to Swiss neutrality. The reason for this change of front was that they too set store by a firmer establishment of the Bourbons on their throne.

Without prejudice to Swiss neutrality, military capitulations were also concluded with other Powers, especially with Holland. The protestant Swiss had always enjoyed Dutch service, but now even catholic cantons came to terms with the kingdom of the Netherlands since catholic Belgium had been joined to Holland in 1815. Switzerland had henceforth to supply more than 10,000 men to the restored House of Orange. Further, Swiss mercenaries, though in much smaller numbers, were in the service of Spain, the Vatican, Naples and England.

It was Prussia, the north German power, and England which took upon themselves to maintain the balance between Austria and French influence in Switzerland. In actual fact the Prussian minister in Switzerland filled a very important position as intermediary, due in part to his own high personal standing, in part to the prestige of the Prussia of Frederick the Great. It was known that Prussia was pursuing no selfish aims in Switzerland, if only because she was so far away. Further, owing to the fact that Neuchatel was subject to the Prussian throne, the relations between Prussia and the Diet were particularly close. The standing of the British embassy was almost as great for similar reasons. It was also assumed that England had no self-seeking aims in Switzerland, while the Legation was in the hands of a minister who commanded great respect, namely Stratford Canning. Switzerland already felt that England was withdrawing from the policy of the Holy Alliance, that she was beginning to protect the liberal parties on the continent, and hence could offer Switzerland invaluable support against Austrian demands.

England and Prussia realized that Swiss neutrality must be an armed power if it was to make itself respected. Stratford Canning, therefore, as early as 1815, submitted a detailed report to the Confederate Commission for military reform, in which he pointed óut the necessity of founding a Swiss military academy, a permanent military authority and a national war fund. The Prussian minister also advised the Swiss to reorganize their army. It was only when, as a result of these suggestions, the " General Army Regulations " were passed by the Diet that Swiss neutrality was no longer a scrap of paper.

How little value was attached to Swiss neutrality in other countries, however, can be seen in General Sebastiani's onslaught in the French chambre. In 1820 he declared that " the times were past when the defence of the eastern frontier of France could be entrusted to a second-rate power " : in the event of war, Switzerland should be at once occupied. It is easy to understand that this standpoint, publicly expressed and unopposed in

France, aroused great indignation in Switzerland. A number of the most prominent Swiss diplomats and military writers published pamphlets on the nature of Swiss neutrality and reminded Europe of its inviolability ; among them were Pictet de Rougemont, Cesar de la Harpe, General Jomini and Colonel Johannes Wieland. This discussion was valuable, firstly because it demonstrated Switzerland's determination to hold fast, whatever happened, to the neutrality she had so hardly won, and secondly because those most competent to do so confirmed the belief that she was capable of defending her neutrality by armed force.

At the moment such confirmation was highly necessary, for the ministers of the reactionary powers in Switzerland were adopting an increasingly overbearing tone. Looking back, it is strange to see how the foreign diplomatic corps in Switzerland at that time was luxuriating and using all the arts of a superior culture to win over the magistrates of the Confederation to their side. Compared with the diplomatic world at Berne the representation of Switzerland abroad was more than humble. For reasons of economy, the Confederation had a representative only in Paris and Vienna, and he was no more than a *chargé d'affaires*. The consequences were firstly that the Swiss authorities were very inadequately informed about the high politics which were made in the European capitals, and hence had to depend on information given by a foreign minister. Further, the one-sidedness of this diplomatic representation gave the foreign ministers at Berne an extraordinary importance because all business passed through their hands and because the Swiss authorities could only negotiate with their governments through them.

The Swiss Diet was no longer courted by the foreign ministers for the sake of the troops it had to give or to refuse to their enemies. What the ministers had to do now was to make the small state of Switzerland tractable to the aims of the great Powers they represented. To reach their goal more easily, the ministers, whenever possible, would present themselves in a body, for Switzerland yielded more readily to united representations. By these methods, such strong pressure was brought to bear on Switzerland in the 1820's that her sovereignty was gravely infringed. A period set in during which the Confederation stood under the tutelage of the Powers, so that the independence it had enjoyed, and the neutrality so closely related to it, suffered seriously.

This tutelage originated with the leading ministers of state. In the same way as after the Peace of Utrecht in the 18th century, an attempt was made after 1815 to maintain the peace of Europe by periodical meetings of the leading statesmen of the five great powers. Metternich, with the help of these meetings, sought to obtain general recognition of his conservative social policy. One of the worst aspects of this policy of restoration was the suppression of any movement for spiritual and political liberty, which became familiar to Switzerland more especially in the form of the persecution of the demagogues.

Metternich's dread of revolution was not quite groundless. There is no question that this movement among the German students had been caught up in republican currents and that those circles were playing with the idea of assassinating the tyrants and liberating the people by force. When Germany set about arresting the members of the Young Germany movement, a number of them fled to Switzerland. Revelations of their intrigues gave the Powers the opportunity of proceeding against Switzerland on pretext of defending the law.

Some of the cantonal grammar schools and the university of Basle gave appointments to German refugees whose presence in Switzerland acted as a leaven of liberalism. The cantonal governments which did so were mainly concerned with getting competent teachers. They may also have been moved in part by compassion and in some cases even by their sympathy with the fearless defenders of libertarian ideas. But to assume that the cantonal governments had any feeling of solidarity with the ideas of the teachers they had appointed would be a crass misunderstanding of their spirit. This error of judgment on the part of the outside world could only arise from the boundless dread of revolution, fanned by the exaggerated and distorted accounts of the doings of the refugees provided by spies and agents provocateurs. Switzerland could not understand what terrible danger threatened the existence of the Powers from the handful of refugees she respected as men of honour.

Metternich's first step was to remind the President of the Diet in 1820 of the solidarity of all governments against revolution. When that proved fruitless, he had two sharp notes presented to the *Vorort* of the Confederation by a united intervention of Austria, Prussia and Russia. In the first, the Powers demanded the instant expulsion of all the refugees who had carried the Piedmont rising into Switzerland. The second contained a most violent attack on the Swiss press, stating that, under cover of the cantonal freedom of the press, it had spread abroad the most distorted and slanderous accounts of the Congresses of Troppau and Laibach. The feeling against Switzerland seemed to reach its culminating point after the Congress of Verona. It exploded in a verbal note from Metternich, in which Switzerland was charged with " having suffered the forbidden presence of criminal societies and military gangs " and categorically required to expel them forthwith. Should Switzerland not comply, she would run the risk of losing her right to neutrality. We find here the new interpretation of Swiss neutrality which the Powers were to apply from that time on. According to Metternich, Switzerland was independent solely by the grace of the great Powers. If she forfeited that grace, she could no longer count on the recognition of her neutrality by the guarantors of her independence, an inference which was highly dangerous for the Swiss right of asylum, the exercise of which was thus placed entirely at the discretion of the Powers.

Under the pressure of these threats, the Diet, in spite of its vivid memories of the gallant struggle for the Swiss right of asylum, took decisions which have entered history under the name of the Press and Aliens' Conclusum. The *Vorort* of the Confederation had now to consent to more drastic police measures against aliens and the censorship of the press. Refugee agitators were expelled, silence was imposed on clamorous editors, and in isolated cases recalcitrant newspapers were suppressed. The Conclusum did not, however, amount to a suspension of the liberty of the press and the right of asylum, but only to a restriction of both. It is not for us to blame that generation for lack of national backbone. The Diet had every reason to believe that it could forestall an armed intervention by the great Powers by a voluntary restriction of the liberty of the press and the right of asylum. Besides, the conscience of the cantons was by no means so clear on the charges brought by the Powers as was later imagined. They knew perfectly well that tolerated refugees were carrying on political agitation against other countries and that certain papers had published attacks on foreign powers which transgressed the bounds of a free press. It was only by bringing active influence to bear on the cantons through decisions binding on all that the little Confederate ship of state could be piloted through the hazardous high seas of European politics. And that end was temporarily gained without any great sacrifice of the National dignity. Public opinion settled down so quietly that the Diet of 1829 was able to withdraw the Press and Aliens' Conclusum without any official notice being taken abroad.

Chapter 10

INTERNAL THREATS TO SWISS NEUTRALITY

As late as 1827, the Austrian minister in Switzerland felt able to assure his Chancellor that the internal condition of the country would remain unchanged unless subjected to some violent shock from the outside. The revolution of 1830 provided the shock. The July Revolution, however, affected Switzerland not only internally but externally also. Thus it was of the gravest import for her independence and neutrality, and that in three respects. Firstly, the Quadruple Alliance was broken ; the French move towards England created something like a European equilibrium, a distribution of weight which agrees well with Swiss neutrality. Secondly, the national regeneration resulting from the revolution in France strengthened the self-confidence of the Confederation and Swiss national feeling. Last but not least, it was these impulses which inspired the liberal leaders and gave them great effective power. On the other hand, the European revolution had awakened hostility to neutrality in the Confederation itself, a danger which threatened its existence as seriously as the previous tutelage of the great Powers.

The gravest peril to Swiss neutrality came from the idea, propagated especially by refugees, that Switzerland must take sides in the European struggle for the great ideals of humanity. She could not stand aside in the conflict between the sovereignty of the people and despotism, for that was the name given to the opposition between liberals and conservatives. Her free constitution imposed upon her the obligation of supporting the peoples of Europe against their governments. This way of thinking, developed with doctrinaire logic, naturally led to the demand that Switzerland should abandon her neutrality in favour of an international democracy. The theory bears every trace of its origin among refugees, those harried and uprooted intellectuals, so many of whom had been cast up on the shores of their Swiss asylum by the waves of European revolution. But even the extreme wing of Swiss liberals refused to countenance dogmas which might loosen the bond of their national existence, and actually turned on them with violence, even when presented in the guise of an enlightened nationalism. It was in this way, for instance, that Mazzini, the arch-conspirator, in his total misapprehension of the Swiss mentality, strove to make his doctrine of intervention palatable to the Confederation. But the Swiss recognized only too well the wolf in sheep's clothing.

Incessantly the exiles preached their doctrine of Switzerland's mission of revolution. The very men who charged their land of refuge with being the accomplice of the great Powers were trying to make it the handmaid of international revolution. The most outstanding contribution to the press agitation against Swiss neutrality is Mazzini's *Neutralità*, published in 1835. Here the Italian, with his purely deductive reasoning, proves how utterly he has failed to grasp the nature of Swiss neutrality. It is not only nonsensical, he declares, but immoral. Wildly over-estimating the importance of Switzerland, he hoped that a declaration of war by the Confederation against royalist Europe would provoke revolution in Germany and Italy.

The exiles, however, did not rest content with literary attacks on Swiss neutrality. Secure on Swiss soil, they conspired against the outside world and planned armed raids into the neighbouring royalist districts with the object of overthrowing the governments in power. The first opportunity was given by the Poles. It is well known how, after the suppression of the Warsaw rising (1830), Polish fugitives poured into the west of Europe in torrents, spreading unrest which was only with difficulty held in check by the governments of the countries in which they found asylum. The Poles interned in the east of France formed a project of going to the help of the republics in an attempted rising at Frankfort. They set out in secret, but learned on the way that the Frankfort rising had failed. Since they had cut off their own retreat by revolutionary proclamations, they promptly turned into Switzerland, some five hundred in number, most of them officers.

A wave of sympathy went out from Swiss liberal circles to the "unhappy victims of despotism." The Poles at once realized the strong position this gave them in Swiss public opinion. Berne was generous in its grant of asylum, and avoided any unnecessary harshness. There the Poles fell under the spell of Mazzini. He saw in the Polish refugees a unique opportunity for putting his plans into action. He made it clear to their leaders that the European revolution must start with revolution in Sardinia, and thus won their support for an armed raid into Piedmont. In January, 1834, the Poles assembled in secret and attempted to enter Savoy in two columns starting from Nyon and Geneva. But the expedition came to a pitiable, not to say ridiculous end. After long negotiations Berne again consented to admit the refugees.

But that was not the end of the affair as far as the outside world was concerned. Austria attempted to take advantage of the scandalous Savoy expedition to establish a strict control of Switzerland and to clear it of all refugees. In Paris, Metternich submitted a proposal for surrounding Switzerland with a military cordon until she expelled all the exiles. But neither London nor Paris agreed. Without any realization of the difficulties of the Swiss situation, Austria, later joined by Baden, Wurtemberg, Bavaria, Sardinia, and even distant Naples, bombarded

Switzerland with notes imperiously demanding the expulsion of the refugees. In its reply the *Vorort* repudiated any charge of having neglected the duties imposed on it by international law, especially of having participated in the Polish expedition. In these transactions we can hear on the Swiss side a note of self-reliance which had never made itself heard during the time of the Restoration.

Metternich now actually demanded a guarantee that there should be no repetition in the future of such incidents as the raid on Savoy. It would seem as if the reiteration of such demands would, in the end, have worn down the resistance of the *Vorort* had it not found support in England and France. The British Premier made no secret of his disapproval of the Austrian *démarche*, and France defended the Swiss Directoire against its enemies at home and abroad. At last the diplomatic storm died away. Switzerland cannot be acquitted of some guilt in the matter, if only on account of a certain negligence in the treatment of the refugees, but she had weathered the storm while maintaining her traditional right of asylum and even without binding herself to a precise definition and interpretation of a somewhat vague notion.

Up to that time, Metternich, in his policy of a Switzerland under tutelage, had always encountered the resistance, open or covert, of the French July monarchy. Towards the middle of the 1830's, however, Louis Philippe's government, alarmed by republican risings, began to substitute a policy of extreme conservatism for its previous republicanism. In foreign policy, that meant a rapprochement with Metternich's system. The ring of great Powers round Switzerland, which had slackened a few years before, now threatened to tighten up again, a development which could not but be prejudicial to the Swiss policy of neutrality.

Switzerland was first made to feel the change in the trend of French policy by the incident of the Articles of

Baden. This was a liberal church programme set up by seven cantons. France interfered tactlessly in this, a purely internal affair, and thus outraged the growing national feeling of Switzerland. When the Swiss liberals attempted to avenge the insult in the Conseil incident, the work of a French *agent provocateur*, Louis Philippe sent troops to the frontier and ordered a strict blockade of Switzerland. England attempted to bring about a reconciliation by reminding Paris of the obligations undertaken by the Powers to respect the integrity and neutrality of Switzerland. The most serious attack on Swiss neutrality was launched by Louis Philippe when he called upon the Confederation to expel Louis Napoleon, who was then living as an exile in the canton of Thurgovie, and again sent a French army corps to the Swiss frontier. In order to spare Switzerland further hardship, the pretender left the country of his own accord.

These repeated attacks on Swiss independence strengthened the feeling for absolute neutrality in the Confederation. Now that not only Austria, but its old friend France was tampering with Swiss sovereignty, any lingering illusions vanished and the necessity of a sober and practical neutrality policy was at last fully realized. The military threats to Switzerland brought home to all concerned both the dangers of international party politics and the dubiousness of the neutrality guarantees of 1815. Trained in the school of foreign political upheavals, liberalism put away its youthful romanticism and learned to reckon with the real forces of European politics. The Swiss feeling for neutrality emerged purified and strengthened from the struggles of the 1830's.

Chapter 11

DEFENCE OF NEUTRALITY IN THE STRUGGLE FOR FEDERAL REFORM

Ever since the movement for the revision of the Federal constitution had been gaining ground, the familiar suspicions of Switzerland had again been growing. The Powers agreed that Switzerland must abide by the traditional federal system. Not that they were honestly convinced that the federal structure best fitted the policy of Switzerland, but the liberals were actively working for the unification of the Confederation and the Powers feared that a central government working in that spirit might offer unwelcome resistance. A firm federal government, they rightly assumed, would have greater power of self-defence against foreign protection. If the Powers had really been aiming at a stricter application of the Swiss policy of neutrality, they would of necessity have promoted the centralization of the Confederation, for they could not but realize that a stronger federal power would be better able to force the Confederate principle of neutrality on refractory cantons.

The Powers now began to insist that in the Vienna treaty of 1815 they had only guaranteed Switzerland as a federal union. Should Switzerland herself amend that constitution, the recognition of her neutrality would also expire, a completely senseless conjunction of two quite unrelated things which Switzerland consistently refused to admit. The policy of the Powers was as self-contradictory as their reasoning. Instead of strengthening the Federal Pact they seriously discredited it in Swiss eyes by repeated interventions. Even non-radical, but patriotic Swiss now felt obliged, from motives of national dignity and self-assertion, to work for a uniform federal state with a stronger executive power. For it was only by way of a revision of the federal constitution that that famous clause in the acts of neutrality which insisted on the freedom of Switzerland from foreign influence could at last become a reality.

Metternich repeatedly reminded Switzerland that her integrity and guaranteed neutrality were only valid as long as the Federal Pact of 1815 remained in force intact. Should that condition no longer hold, the Powers would revoke their consent to the Declaration of Vienna. It was from this standpoint that Metternich dealt both with the question of the dissolution of the monasteries in Argovie and the Sonderbund. The latter, which began with raids on the federalistic and catholic old cantons of Switzerland by armed radicals, was certainly an internal affair, but as a huge threat to peace and public order, capable of plunging the country into chaos, it also involved the external situation of Switzerland. This armed party conflict had even made it doubtful whether neutrality could be maintained. For Metternich, it was a matter of principle which had to be solved by a principle. By reducing radicalism, the principle of evil, to silence, he also hoped to bring about a purge of Switzerland from the exiles.

At Metternich's instigation the three eastern Powers presented Berne with notes couched in the same terms, declaring the continued existence of the Federal Pact to be the condition of friendly relations in the future. Ochsenbein, the President of the Diet, answered that Berne must request the Powers to desist from any attempt at interference. He was able to take this bold line because he knew that the Powers were not united among themselves. In the meantime, however, Guizot, the French Premier, completed the re-orientation of his foreign policy which brought him into line with Austria and tallied with his new and conservative policy in home affairs. It is more than doubtful whether Switzerland could have resisted this union of her two most powerful neighbours if England had not begun to take an interest in the Swiss situation as part of the central European question. To anticipate a little, without strong support from England, Switzerland could hardly have carried out the reform of the Confederation with so little molestation.

England's foreign policy at that time was entirely in the hands of Palmerston. It would not be just to call it definitely liberal : it was realist and opportunist. It would be over-sentimental to see in Palmerston's support of Switzerland any far-reaching agreement of his political views with those of the Swiss radicals. While we cannot deny a certain undertone of friendliness in the relations between the two countries, Palmerston's attitude was nevertheless mainly determined by motives of pure interest. England required peace in central Europe if her trade and commerce were to flourish. If Switzerland provided a pretext for an armed intervention by Austria and France, a great struggle in central Europe might very well ensue. This latent danger would be most likely to vanish if the power of the Confederation in Switzerland were to outgrow all foreign influence. It was only as an independent, inviolable territory that Switzerland could play the part assigned to her of buffer-state between Austria and France. That was the value of Swiss independence and neutrality for Palmerston's policy. It was for the same reasons that he so tenaciously resisted any attempt at intervention in Swiss affairs. Since Palmerston's foreign policy had the support of the whole of the British nation, it looked as if English public opinion had taken sides for Switzerland.

In the notorious speech with which he opened the July Diet of 1847, Ochsenbein took advantage of the occasion to reply to foreign interpretations of Swiss neutrality. While the continental powers were highly indignant at this provocative speech, Palmerston sent him his congratulations. Palmerston avoided making any definite statement on the Swiss affair to the Powers. He eluded all commitments, but by an adroit, even daring policy, gradually succeeded in getting the control of the whole diplomatic machinery into his hands. With telegrams and special missions to the Diet, he worked for a peaceful solution to the conflict on the grounds that nothing was more terrible in any country than civil war ; an attack on the Sonderbund would provoke an intervention by the Powers.

In actual fact Guizot was preparing an intervention by the great Powers and submitted to them a note on the subject, basing the right to intervene, among other things, on the neutrality guarantee. Palmerston produced a counter-proposal, whereupon, on November 20th, 1847, an identical note was at last drafted. According to this final draft, the Sonderbund was itself to request the Pope to withdraw the Jesuits from Switzerland. Further, the sovereignty of all cantons was to be guaranteed and the Federal constitution only to be amended with the consent of all the cantons. Palmerston had also stipulated that a rejection of this settlement should not lead to an armed intervention by the Powers.

A great deal of time was taken up in these diplomatic transactions. The Sonderbund had to abandon any hope of a timely intervention by the Powers. The armed assistance expected from France and Austria failed to put in an appearance. The Swiss army, however, acted promptly and to the point, so that military victories followed hard on each others' heels. Fribourg fell on November 14th, Lucerne on November 24th, without any concerted action by the Powers. Palmerston, by dint of his superior diplomacy, had succeeded in delaying their intervention.

When Palmerston handed over the note of mediation,

he had entrusted his representative, Stratford Canning, with an extraordinary mission. When Canning arrived at Berne, however, the civil war was already over, so that he refrained from presenting it. On November 30th, however, the representatives of France, Austria and Prussia presented identical notes. The fact that England had withdrawn from this united note after first having persuaded them to moderate its terms aroused great indignation among the intervening Powers. The note presented could hardly have been in more glaring contrast to the actual facts, and was therefore self-condemned. For the war council of the Sonderbund, to which it was addressed, no longer existed, the pretended unanimity among the five Powers was a fiction and there was no kind of military dispute to be settled. Hence the Diet found no difficulty in replying. With almost insulting sarcasm it thanked the Powers for their offer of intervention, which was based on the assumption of a state of war which no longer existed. Moreover, mediation from outside was at variance with the position of Switzerland as established by treaty as well as with the Federal constitution.

For all the tone of elation in the note, there was no complaint of breaches of neutrality by France and Austria. Within the Diet, however, they were sharply censured. The close relations between the Powers and the Sonderbund, and the constant encouragement and secret advice they gave to it, were in themselves unneutral. It was also a breach of formal neutrality for Austria to grant the Sonderbund a loan without interest and to send it 3,000 rifles and ammunition from the arsenal at Milan. It was further a breach of neutrality for France to send guns from Besancon and for Sardinia to sell arms. But since the continental governments had sided with the Sonderbund, it was not worth while making particular mention of unneutral behaviour. The Powers, however,

F

were by no means disposed to accept the snub from the Diet and to recognize the *fait accompli* in Switzerland. They handed the central government of the Confederation a further note in which they demanded the integrity of cantonal sovereignty. The Federal constitution could only be amended by the unanimous consent of all the members of the Confederation. The Powers inferred their right to put forward this demand from the treaties of 1815. Once again they preached on Metternich's text—that the Powers had only granted territorial expansion and permanent neutrality to Switzerland in those treaties in consideration of the final conclusion of the Federal Pact.

Meanwhile, owing to the revolution, the Powers had lost their taste for intervention in Switzerland. The way in which Switzerland was reconstituting herself deprived them of any plausible reason for doing so. For the strengthening of the central power of the Confederation gave promise of greater consistency in the application of the right of asylum, indeed, of a stricter application of the policy of neutrality as a whole. In the hands of Burgomaster Furrer of Zurich, who had been entrusted with the drafting of the answer to the Powers, it grew into a state document which can hardly be equalled in diplomatic records for diplomatic tact, clear thinking and persuasive power. It was the first time that a politically responsible authority had given so generally valid an historical and legal interpretation to the acts of neutrality. This impressive document brought to a close a period of vagueness and vacillation in neutral feeling and of uninterrupted threats to, or breaches of, Swiss sovereignty. At the same time it opened the way to a more vigorous, clearer policy of neutrality.

Chapter 12

PRESERVATION OF SWISS NEUTRALITY AT THE TIME OF
THE NATIONAL WARS OF LIBERATION

Before the Confederation had had time to re-constitute
itself, the triumphant Diet was assailed on every hand
by the temptation to put its old ideals of freedom and the
solidarity of the people into action by taking part in the
general revolution. It is therefore of the greatest importance that the Diet, for all its elation, should have been
able to preserve the strictest abstinence and, at this very
moment, to lay down the lines of its future foreign policy.
That policy was entirely directed towards neutrality and
humaneness in the granting of asylum, which amounted,
in actual fact, to non-intervention. It is a proof of how
deeply the old political principle was rooted in the minds
of the people that it emerged intact from the revolutionary
storms of the spring of 1848. Realizing that the national
existence depended on its maintenance, the radical
leaders, for its sake, refrained from any attempt to put
into action the ideas they had proclaimed not only in
confidential conversation, but before the public. They
made this sacrifice of their dearest wishes out of a deeper
insight into the vital necessities of the country and an
increased sense of responsibility to the union of states they
administered. A cirular letter from Berne, the *Vorort*, to all
the cantons expressed this statesmanlike view with the
greatest emphasis.

Hardly had Berne given this fresh expression to the
basic principle of Swiss foreign policy when the Diet,
confronted with the offer of an alliance, had to declare
whether the rule was to be absolute. King Charles Albert
of Sardinia, who had recently taken the lead in the
Lombard revolt against Austria, offered to conclude an

offensive and defensive alliance with Switzerland. In a note couched in the most honeyed terms and spattered with fulsome compliments, the Sardinian minister in Switzerland tried to persuade her to abandon her neutrality. This led to a heated and brilliant discussion of the policy of neutrality in the Diet. A considerable minority opposed the rigid maintenance of the traditional conception of neutrality. In the present European struggle, there were principles at stake, the principle of absolutism against the principle of democracy. Democratic freedom had originated in Switzerland. If Switzerland did not come to the help of the peoples which were fighting for their freedom, she would be guilty of self-contradiction. She must, for her own sake, take sides in order that her voice might carry weight in the coming European congress.

In face of this propaganda for the temporary suspension of neutrality in favour of a higher ideal, and in the true interests of Switzerland, the majority of the Diet held unflinchingly to the principle of neutrality in its traditional sense, that is, in the sense of perpetual neutrality. The excitement of victory had not blinded the majority of the radicals to a just estimate of the relative greatness of the European Powers, nor had they forgotten that in politics, party passion must give way to dispassionate reflection and consideration for the good of the state. Their feeling for the Confederation as a whole had not been stifled ; they still realized that the salvation of Switzerland lay in abstinence in foreign politics and the absence of territorial aims, and it is a testimony to their sense of right that they refused to take advantage of the misfortunes of their neighbours. Their practical common sense was not to be taken in by the dubious schemes of Piedmont, of which they had had more than one experience in the past. The lesson these men were able to learn from history shows how free they were of any illusions as to the preservation of their neutrality. Not the assurances of foreign Powers but their own strength was its safeguard.

While Switzerland remained neutral towards Sardinia-Piedmont, there was a breach of neutrality by the canton of Ticino in favour of the Italian revolutionaries. In this canton, the neighbour of Lombardy, and of the same race and tongue, the movement of liberation caught fire so fiercely that the neutral policy of the central government of the Confederation could not quite hold its own. The canton had long been the favourite asylum of the Lombard revolutionaries. Not only were the political refugees readily admitted ; they found active support among the Ticinese and the radicals. Lugano was even regarded as the fountain head of the revolutionary propaganda in Lombardy.

When the rising in Lombardy broke out on March 19th, 1848, some 700 Ticinese volunteers, in small groups, set out across the frontier for Milan. After the Sardinian defeat at Custozza, parts of the beaten army fled back into the Grisons and the Ticino. Their number may have been 20,000 in all. Although for the time being no further serious violation of the frontier occurred, on September 15th, Radetzky, the Austrian commander in Lombardy, expelled all Ticinese from Lombardy and suspended postal and commercial communications with Switzerland. These severe measures were in the main provoked by the participation of the Ticinese volunteers in the Milan rising. They aroused exaggerated bitterness in the Ticino and poisoned relations with Austria for a long time to come. This was the state of feeling which helped the refugees to commit a further breach of neutrality. For long past, Mazzini had been organizing a rising in Lombardy from the Ticino. It broke out prematurely in October, and a large number of exiles hurried to join it in secret.

This led to a severe crisis between the central government of the Confederation and the canton of Ticino. Confederate groups advanced into the Ticino and the canton felt that it was being treated like an occupied country. A commission of the National Council confirmed the steps taken by the representatives of the Confederation, by which all Italian refugees were to be removed from the Ticino and interned in central Switzerland. Caught thus between the devil of Austria and the deep sea of the Confederation, the Ticino, gnashing its teeth, submitted to the decisions of the Federal Assembly. The Council of States expelled all male refugees of over eighteen years of age from the canton, and only granted newcomers leave to remain for one week.

In the succeeding years, the Ticinese never ceased to take a lively share in the Italian revolutionary movements, thus provoking constant friction with Austria. No Swiss canton had more difficulty in submitting to the guidance of the Federal Council in matters of foreign policy, nor did any so seriously obstruct the Council's neutrality policy. Though the Federal Council yielded to the pressure of the great Powers, especially to that of Austria, one thing it steadfastly refused—to repatriate revolutionaries.

The plight of Swiss neutrality was no less serious in the north than in the south. There too the Swiss population sympathized with the revolutionary aims of their racial brothers across the frontier. For years there had been relations between the German and the Swiss liberals, and those relations had been strengthened by political refugees during the revolution. When revolutionary risings were afoot in the neighbouring grand duchy of Baden in 1848, Berne reminded the cantons of their strict neutrality. The frontier cantons called out their men, not only to prevent the entry of defeated troops, but more especially against the German revolutionaries who were planning to cross the frontier from Alsace and to invade Germany from Switzerland. Baden had actually counted on armed help from Switzerland. Only after a few hundred German workmen had hurried to the help of the Baden rising from Switzerland, and the Swiss troops had prevented them from crossing the frontier armed and *en masse*, had neutrality been preserved. It is true that arms had been smuggled into the city of Basle from the Basle country districts, but when the Swiss troops discovered the transports they were confiscated.

The second rising in Baden blew over so quickly that it was unnecessary for the Confederation to man the frontiers. On the other hand, the third rising and the ensuing riots in the Bavarian Palatinate became dangerous. Once there were skirmishes between the rioters and the German troops close to the Swiss frontier, and several hundred Germans again left Switzerland to join the insurgents in Baden. In view of the impending and serious danger, the Federal Council sent 5,000 Swiss troops to the northern frontier. After the defeat of the Baden democrats, over 9,000 of the beaten troops entered Switzerland with war material of all kinds. The gravest threat to Swiss neutrality, however, lay in the presence of a large and victorious Prussian army in the neighbourhood of the frontier. It was feared in Switzerland, and not without cause, that Prussia might take advantage of the victory over the revolution in Baden and the Palatinate to suppress the revolution in Neuchatel and re-establish the monarchy there. As we now know, the danger of a Prussian invasion was greater than even the most pessimistic radicals imagined at the time. It was only prevented by the objections of the great Powers.

Before Prussia had even abandoned the idea of a passage of arms with Switzerland, the Federal Council resolved on a regulation of the refugee question which should be binding on the whole country. It expelled the political and military leaders of the third Baden rising. Since this decision aroused great indignation in Switzerland, the Federal Council consented to amend it. In the midst of the troubles caused by the still unsolved refugee question, there was a violation of Swiss neutrality on the northern frontier near the Baden enclave of Busingen. This moved the Federal Council to increase the frontier troops to a strength of 25,000 men and to place General Dufour in temporary command. The conflict was then peaceably settled.

The refugee question, however, was causing growing excitement. At the beginning of 1850 a conference took place in Paris between the representatives of France, Prussia and Austria to discuss an ultimatum to Switzerland demanding the immediate expulsion of all refugees. Both Germany and France had already gone so far as to move troops up to the Swiss frontier. An attack on the Confederation was expected everywhere ; its situation was far more serious than it had been for instance, in the autumn of 1847. But the Paris conference arrived at no binding conclusions. The Federal Council strained every nerve to obtain an amnesty for the refugees from their home countries, or at least to facilitate their emigration to England or America. Thus about the middle of 1851, the number of refugees had been reduced to a few hundred.

Two years later Switzerland was again involved in a serious dispute with Austria, though this time the Federal Council refused to be intimidated. In the end, Austria gave way, for one thing on account of the outbreak of troubles in the East. Although the Crimean war was waged far away from Switzerland, the Federal Council considered it necessary to remind the cantons of their strict neutrality. The radicals, which means the overwhelming majority of the Swiss population, nevertheless warmly espoused the cause of England, which is hardly surprising in view of the ideal aims England was pursuing in the war and the friendly attitude she showed to the Federal Council. Under the eyes of the Federal authorities, English officers illegally recruited 3,300 men for the " British Swiss Legion," which did not, however, reach the theatre of war. The enlistment of some 700 men in France was no breach of neutrality since it was done by private enterprise. Faithful to her principle of not participating in guarantee treaties, Switzerland refused an invitation by the Congress of Paris in 1856 to join in a convention for the prevention of future conflicts.

Chapter 13

THE EFFECT OF FOREIGN WARS ON THE DIFFERENTIATION
OF NEUTRALITY

While Switzerland was imagining that she could now
devote her entire attention to urgent economic questions,
her neutrality was suddenly and gravely threatened,
for reasons of home and foreign policy, by Prussia, now
one of the leading European Powers. The occasion arose
from the very curious legal and political relation which
had existed between the canton of Neuchatel and the
Confederation since 1815. At that time the canton had
been incorporated in the Confederation as an equal
member, yet had remained bound to the Prussian
monarchy. A hybrid relation of such a kind could remain
harmless as long as conditions in Europe and the Confederation were undisturbed. The rise of the democratic
movement, however, went hand in hand with the
tendency to break away from Prussia. When the February
revolution of 1848 broke out in France, the democrats of
Neuchatel were the first to respond. They proclaimed a
republic and were adopted as a full member of the new
Confederation. Frederick William IV of Prussia, however,
did not abandon his principality. His adherents rose in
counter-revolution in September, 1856, but were arrested.
The king of Prussia demanded their liberation, which the
Federal Council only promised on condition that Frederick
William first surrendered all claims to Neuchatel.

This dispute quickly swelled into a dangerous conflict
which kept the European cabinets on the *qui vive* for the
whole winter of 1856-1857. The neighbour Powers of the
Confederation supported the Prussian intervention in so
far as, taking their stand on the treaties of 1815, they did
not admit Switzerland's right to break the connection

between Neuchatel and Prussia on her own account. Among the signatories of the Vienna treaties, England alone had consistently reminded the King of Prussia of the guaranteed neutrality of Switzerland. When Frederick William put the Prussian army under arms and entered into negotiations with the south German states for the right of passage, when war between Prussia and Switzerland seemed imminent, the English cabinet put the Prussian government under unprecedented diplomatic pressure : " Moreover Prussia was a party to all the arrangement of 1815, by which the neutrality, the independence and the inviolability of Switzerland are placed under the guarantee of all the Powers who are parties to the Treaties of that year. The hostile proceedings contemplated by the King would therefore not only be a subject of painful regret to the community of the European nations, but would also be at variance with positive engagements taken by Prussia towards all the other Powers who are contracting parties to those engagements."

The commander of the Swiss armies, General Dufour, had conceived the bold plan of abandoning the defensive and, in order to save the canton of Schaffhouse which, lying on the farther bank of the Rhine was in an untenable position, of marching to meet the approaching enemy and thus carrying the war into the south of Germany. In Switzerland this was not regarded as unneutral, but as an emergency action undertaken to avert a threat to her neutrality. In the end, matters did not go so far as this extreme step. At the last moment, the mediating Powers, England and France, were able to bring about a settlement by which Switzerland liberated the imprisoned royalists and the king finally abandoned all claim to his principality of Neuchatel.

The great advantage for Switzerland was that she had not had to buy this settlement at the cost of her neutrality.

A dangerous constitutional anomaly, which was a perpetual temptation to unneutral interventions, had vanished from the Confederation. Neutral Switzerland had commanded the respect of the whole of Europe. The great wave of popular feeling, the most unanimous Switzerland had seen for centuries, had shown that the new federal state could protect its neutrality better than the old federation of states.

It was only to be expected that the union of Italy should arouse sympathy in Switzerland. Feeling, however, did not rise so high as in 1848. For now Italy was setting about the establishment of a kingdom of Italy, and not of a democratic republic, and the struggle was for power rather than principles. The movement was led by Napoleon III, a renegade from liberalism, and Switzerland had little to hope from his policy of territorial expansion. Even the most zealous partisans of the solidarity of the peoples now regarded the strictest neutrality as the " only practical policy." When Cavour, in a note to the Federal Council, expressed his hope that Switzerland would observe a " benevolent neutrality " towards Sardinia, the Federal Council, with some asperity, replied : " If the Italian people cannot discriminate between motives of neutrality and expedience, their governments at any rate might appreciate the distinction." And when an irredentist proclamation in Milan invited the Ticinese to dissolve their " curious and unlovely bond with Switzerland," the Ticinese member of the Federal Council could quietly point to the united front presented by all the Ticinese parties to " the common enemy."

The struggle cast 650 scattered Austrians over the frontier into Switzerland. By a convention, they were admitted but disarmed and conducted into the interior of the country. This convention had been drawn up on the basis of a detailed instruction in which the Federal Council had carefully considered every possibility of an

intervention and the measures to be taken against it.
This instruction is the more important in that, for the first
time in Europe, the procedure for the internment of troops
in flight in international wars was defined in detail. It is
no accident that this development of international law
should have taken place in Switzerland. For a differential
practice in the granting of asylum to political refugees
had already developed there, which the Federal Council
was able to use as a standard. The Federal Council
succeeded in obtaining the consent of the Powers to these
basic regulations (disarming and removal to the interior
of the country). It was particularly anxious that the
internment of troops in flight should be regarded as a free
right of the neutral state and not as an obligation
incumbent upon it. Therefore, in its opinion, the cost
of the maintenance of the internees should be borne by
the state to which troops entering neutral territory
belonged. The Federal Council's view of the question
prevailed. It was adopted by the Brussels Conference
of 1874 and confirmed by the two peace Congresses at
the Hague in 1899 and 1907. The Powers also recognized
the right of Switzerland to repatriate internees before the
end of the war provided guarantee was given that the
repatriates should not be used again in the same war.

The Italian war resulted in a further differentiation of
Swiss neutrality, namely the prohibition of foreign
mercenary service for the whole Confederation. The
Swiss regiments in the service of Naples and the Vatican
were now exposed to such violent attacks that the radicals
wished to put a Confederate embargo on any foreign
service whatever. Since the 18th century, the criticisms
of Swiss mercenary service had never ceased. The fact
that it now swelled to such proportions was due to certain
incidents. King Francis II of Naples was suppressing
the revolutionary movement with the help of his so-called
Swiss regiments, while in the Marches and in Umbria

the Pope was supporting his power against the storm of revolution with Swiss troops. Throughout Italy, popular fury turned on the foreign troops as the most dangerous enemies to *Italia unita*. When a mutiny, for which the Federal Council must bear some responsibility, broke out among the Swiss regiments, the Council had them dismissed and recalled them.

Beyond this practical solution of the question of mercenary service, however, the Federal Council was anxious to find a solution on principle. Even the liberal government in England, by whose views the Federal Council set great store, informed it that mercenary service was prejudicial to the dignity of Switzerland. The Council's draft bill not only prohibited the enlistment of troops, but forbade men to enlist. Its supporters declared that foreign service was a danger to neutrality, its opponents that Switzerland had possessed the acknowledged right for centuries and was, as a state, not responsible for its nationals in foreign service. The law against passive enlistment was passed by an overwhelming majority.

Even at the beginning of the war the Federal Council had contemplated the possibility of the cession of Savoy to France. It gave the French government to understand that the military threat which would arise for Switzerland could only be removed by the cession of the north of Savoy to Switzerland, that is, above all, the provinces of Chablais and Faucigny and part of Genevois. The only rights to the north of Savoy that Switzerland possessed consisted in the fact that, in case of war, she might occupy the zone of Savoy neutralized in 1815. Savoy stood in no constitutional relation to Switzerland, which had only the right to demand that the neutrality of Savoy should be preserved, to whatever state it should fall. But at that time, Switzerland had drawn much more far-reaching conclusions from the treaties, which were in any case not very explicit. She inferred from them something like a right to Savoy. It may be that this was in part due to a fear which Geneva had felt since the time of Louis XIV, and which had been justified at the time of Napoleon, namely that France might take possession of Geneva.

Napoleon III first gave a verbal declaration that it would be a pleasure to him to cede Chablais and Faucigny to Switzerland. That would have been on the lines of the aims of 1815, would have put an end to all confusion and given Geneva room to breathe. For various reasons, however, the Emperor went back on his original intention, but instead of handling the matter with tact and prudence, Switzerland now proceeded to stand on her rights. Active radical circles attempted to drag public opinion into war, but were unable to arouse a united popular movement as in 1857. In their zeal, they began to exaggerate, and set so high a value on the north of Savoy for the neutrality of Switzerland that France might well begin to wonder whether it was not the right thing to keep Savoy in order to get a firmer grip on Switzerland. A protest by the Federal Council to the European great Powers passed unheeded.

In order to avoid giving the annexation of Savoy the appearance of a pure seizure without consideration for the wishes of the population, France organized a plebiscite. Savoy had obtained from the emperor his promise to create a certain free zone in favour of the north of Savoy which would ensure to those districts the free import of Swiss goods. The point at issue was to obtain for those districts the same privileged position as had been given to the Pays de Gex in 1815 and to the small Sardinian zone in the south-east of the canton of Geneva in 1816. The question put to the vote was not, as it should have been : " Do you wish to belong to France or to Switzerland ? " but simply " Do you wish, on condition of customs exemption, to belong to France ? " The nationalist aim of France was identified with the economic advantage of northern Savoy. The vote went clearly against Switzerland, so that France formally took possession of Savoy. The neutrality of Savoy remained.

In the North American civil war, 1861-1865, about 6,000 Swiss were fighting on the side of the Union, Swiss sympathies being overwhelmingly on that side. There were also some thousand Swiss in the armies of the southern states. Many of them were forced into active service by the government. At the end of the war, in 1865, so-called addresses of sympathy streamed into Washington from various sections of the Swiss public. A well-known and widely-read newspaper wrote that it was a point of honour for the whole Swiss nation " not to remain dumb in face of one of the greatest events in the history of the world, but to proclaim unanimously and in no uncertain terms their sympathies for the cause of political and social freedom."

Swiss public opinion was no less outspoken when a rising, which led to great bloodshed, broke out in Russian Poland in 1863. It is true that the Federal Council, as the government of a neutral country, did not join the intervention of the western Powers in favour of the maltreated people. The sympathy felt by the whole population for a nation fighting for its freedom was all the warmer and more active. The liberals pitied the Poles as the victims of czarist despotism, the catholics as persecuted brothers in the faith. A central committee was set up at Zurich which, in defiance of the neutral status of Switzerland, sent arms and munitions to the oppressed Poles. This one-sided partisanship was revenged on the Swiss in Russia.

The speech of the President of the Council of States on the outbreak of the German civil war, however, shows how deeply the principle of strict neutrality was striking root in Switzerland, for he defined any surrender of neutrality as political suicide. On its part the Federal Council quietly took steps to prevent the passage of foreign troops by force. Owing to the short duration of the war it was possible to dismiss the small levy of Swiss troops at the end of ten weeks. The position of Switzerland was greatly changed for the worse by the formation of strong national states to north and south. She was now surrounded by four great Powers all with a bias to conquest. Realizing the greater threat to Switzerland, the Federal Council decided to pursue the completion of the national defences with greater energy.

When France declared war on Germany in July, 1870, it was as yet uncertain whether southern Germany, Austria and Italy would not be drawn into the struggle too, which would have meant an iron ring of belligerent states round Switzerland. In face of this impending danger, five divisions, numbering 37,423 men, were called to the colours, the rest of the levy being left under arms. This extraordinary demonstration of strength made it perfectly clear to the outside world how seriously Switzerland took her neutrality. In order to maintain it more strictly, the Federal Council laid an embargo on any supply of war material and arms to the belligerents. It also reissued the prohibition of the recruitment of troops on Swiss territory. Without actually setting up a censorship, the Council warned the press to remain perfectly impartial.

Towards the end of the war, the French army of the east, under General Bourbaki, was pushed into Switzerland. The terms of the agreement for its entry, as dictated by Switzerland, were—surrender of all arms, equipment and regimental chests. Beginning with February 1st, 1871, over 90,000 French troops were washed up on the saving soil of Switzerland. Bourbaki's army was in a pitiable state of exhaustion and anarchy ; all bonds of discipline and obedience were loosed. The internment of so large and demoralized a body of men presented Switzerland with a serious problem. Rich and poor vied with each other in offers of hospitality, nursing and charity.

Swiss helpfulness, however, was not exhausted by charity. At the request of Bavaria and Baden, the Swiss Legation in Paris took charge of the interests of their subjects and further gave protection and help to all Germans present in Paris. When the storm on Strasburg, an old friend of Switzerland, was imminent, a Swiss aid committee, with the permission of the German command, entered the threatened city and took 2,500 non-combatants—aged, women and children—back into refuge in Switzerland.

While feeling in Switzerland at the beginning of the war was entirely on the side of Germany owing to the old grudge against France, a change soon came. The noisy rejoicings in Germany, who required the Confederation not only to understand, but to join in, alienated a great deal of sympathy. And when a discordant note of desire for Swiss territory began to creep into German self-assertiveness, the Swiss press replied with a sharpness which provoked an unpleasant press war. The German lust of conquest, and the disaster to the neighbour republic of France in its heroic defence, aroused an antipathy to Germany in many circles. There was widespread feeling for France in Switzerland.

On the whole, it was fortunate outward circumstances rather than any trial of her military strength which enabled Switzerland to come through the war safe and sound and to preserve her neutrality absolutely intact.

Chapter 14

MEANING OF NEUTRALITY IN THE AGE OF IMPERIALISM

The notion of power has seldom bloomed so rankly in Europe as in the period which set in between 1870 and 1880. Its native soil was the great Powers, the fully organized constitutional, economic and national bodies. They began to disregard the minor states and to eliminate them from high politics. Indeed, in this period it actually looked as if the Confederation had resigned from world politics. Foreign observers concluded that the absence of territorial aims in Switzerland meant her relinquishment of any foreign policy. There is this much truth in the assumption, that the Swiss man in the street began to regard neutrality as a protective rampart behind which he could go about his business in perfect security. The period of excitability in foreign policy about the middle of the century was followed by one of satiety. Economic life absorbed all energy and all interest. It was as if Switzerland were seeking to recuperate from past shocks in economic prosperity, and hence forgetting the dangers to which she was exposed in the centre of Europe. More and more, people yielded to cosmopolitan ideals ; they found visible expression in a number of international organizations which set up their headquarters in Switzerland. The innate preference of the Swiss for home affairs grew into political introversion. It was only gradually and in the teeth of tenacious opposition that a scanty diplomatic representation abroad could be maintained. The consulates were for the most part honorary posts, while in the Swiss Foreign Office was given the characteristic title of Political Department.

Switzerland was rudely startled out of her repose in foreign affairs by a sharp dispute with Bismark. Her official relations with the German Empire under Bismark were at first entirely correct and friendly. While public opinion in the Confederation was not exactly cordial to Bismark, more especially since the time of the *Kulturkampf*, official relations were unaffected. Far-seeing minds in Switzerland certainly feared very early a disturbance of the European equilibrium by the new conglomeration of power in the north which would be a serious threat to Swiss neutrality. This was the more to be feared as the ruthless Chancellor seemed to be devoid of legal or moral scruples.

The relations between Switzerland and the Empire were put to the first serious test when a large number of German socialists fled to Switzerland after the promulgation of Bismark's famous edicts against the social democrats. They published their main organ at Zurich under the name of the *Sozialdemokrat* and smuggled it into Germany in all kinds of secret ways. Sensational revelations in the Reichstag about the maintenance of German *agents provocateurs* in Switzerland annoyed the Chancellor deeply. He took advantage of an experiment with explosives carried out by Russian anarchists at Zurich to win over the Czar with flimsy suspicions of Switzerland. It was extremely difficult for the Federal Council to reassure the Russian government and to prove the groundlessness of the accusations. The enquiry into the whole affair was not yet concluded when a Prussian police inspector, who was endeavouring to recruit an *agent provocateur* on Swiss territory, was arrested by one of the cantonal governments and expelled from the country by the Federal Council.

For Bismark, this was the last straw. He at once demanded from Switzerland the withdrawal of the order of expulsion, with an apology ; in case of refusal he threatened reprisals. Germany, he declared, would be obliged to set up her own police force on Swiss territory, the Swiss being inadequate. If he were not given satisfaction, he would no longer respect Swiss neutrality. He succeeded in causing Russia and Austria, his co-guarantors of Swiss neutrality, to approach the Federal Council in that sense. The Powers declared that Swiss neutrality carried with it the obligation on the part of the Confederation " to prevent machinations calculated to disturb the peace of their countries, otherwise they would be obliged to examine the question whether Swiss neutrality was still in their interests." This was nothing more nor less than a revival of the old idea, familiar at the time of the Restoration, that Switzerland was pledged to her neighbours for the enjoyment of her neutrality. Should she fail to fulfil her engagements, the Powers were no longer obliged to respect her neutrality.

The Federal Council under Droz repudiated with the greatest precision this false and confused representation of Swiss neutrality, which Switzerland had repeatedly refused to countenance in the course of the 19th century. The supervision and suppression of anarchist plots could not be regarded as an obligation exclusively binding on her and implicit in her neutrality. That obligation was incumbent on every state, neutral or not. Neutrality could not be prejudicial to sovereignty. It was impossible to be neutral in the true sense of the word while in a state of dependence. Even as a neutral state, Switzerland, like every other sovereign state, claimed the right of exercising her police functions on her own territory alone.

In this duel of notes with the Chancellor, the Federal Council had the unanimous support of parliament and the press, while Bismark was unable to rely on united public opinion in his country. It is not clear whether he was seriously contemplating war with Switzerland. In any case, Waldersee, the Chief of the German General Staff, was convinced that Bismark had war in mind and would not let matters rest at closing the frontiers. In the end, however, Bismark himself brushed aside the conflict which he had fanned into a dispute on international law. The fall of the Chancellor, which took place in the following year, greatly facilitated the establishment of lasting good relations between Switzerland and Germany. Swiss judgments of Bismark were unanimous in the repudiation of the idea of power he incorporated. This attitude was characteristically Swiss, for the extremely vulnerable neutrality of the little Confederation surrounded by great Powers can only live if the rule of law is binding on all. The distrust which Switzerland has always felt in the course of her history towards any disturber of the European balance of power turned instinctively against Bismark.

Switzerland was given clearly to understand that, in world politics, she had declined into a mere object of the great Powers. That object now became of great importance owing to its peculiar situation in military strategy. The most important communication between the north and south of central Europe, the Gotthard tunnel, opened in 1882, lay in the territory of the small Swiss state. One of the most important routes between east and west, which had often served as a convenient transit route in the past, also crossed Switzerland. All this gave Switzerland a kind of controlling key-position in the central Alpine region. It can therefore be no matter for surprise if the general staffs of the great Powers repeatedly included Switzerland in their plans. Neutral Switzerland offered all her neighbours highly welcome cover for their flanks. A violation of her neutrality by the other side might prove a blow on a sensitive spot. The high command of every foreign army had to give serious consideration to the question whether the respect or the violation of Swiss neutrality was more to its advantage. Ultimately, all these calculations ended in the question whether Swiss neutrality could be really trusted, that is, whether

Switzerland possessed the unanimous will and the military power to defend her neutrality against threats.

In the general staff conversations of the Triple Alliance the problem of Swiss neutrality loomed the larger as it became clearer that the allies were aiming at turning the political alliance to military ends. It was in the first place Italian military circles which considered the idea of sending troops over the Gotthard to the help of their northern ally in case of war with France. But these plans were consistently repudiated by the political and military leaders of Germany. The German General Staff, through all changes in its personnel, maintained its respect for Swiss neutrality with impressive steadfastness. In Italian military circles, however, the idea of a march through Switzerland was always considered from the conclusion of the Triple Alliance right down to its collapse. The danger to Swiss neutrality vanished only when the plan of a direct military co-operation between Germany and Italy was finally abandoned.

Of France it can be almost as positively asserted that neither her political nor her military leaders contemplated any violation of Swiss neutrality. In the last few years before the outbreak of the first world war, however, the French seem to have had grave fears that the Central Powers, leaving Belfort on one side, might invade France by way of Switzerland. The plan of attack which entered into force in spring, 1914, provided for one army corps which was to invade upper Alsace immediately upon the outbreak of war and destroy the German railway terminus at Basle.

The eagerness with which the authorities of the Confederation took every step to avoid even the appearance of a bias towards the Central Powers betrayed a certain uneasiness. When the Kaiser expressed his wish to be present at the Swiss army manoeuvres, the President of the French Republic was first invited to

Berne in 1910, an event which was staged as a state visit, so that the balance between the two neighbours should on no account be disturbed. In spite of these precautions, rumours of secret military agreements between Switzerland and both Germany and Austria were especially rife in diplomatic military circles in England. From 1909 to 1911 the British military attachés at Rome and Berne sent alarming memoranda on the attitude of Switzerland to the Foreign Office, where they were occasionally believed. It was not until reassuring reports were received from France that Swiss neutrality was dispassionately assessed in London.

It was, however, not only in the foreign general staffs that Swiss neutrality played a quite definite part. It became increasingly important in foreign diplomacy also. Occasionally, in the settlement of international disputes, Swiss intermediaries were called in, since, as citizens of a permanently neutral state, they seemed to offer the best guarantee of impartiality. This happened in the settlement of the inspectorate of Crete and in the question of the Moroccan police. Neutral Swiss territory, moreover, came to be used more and more for the headquarters of international offices, for instance for the post, telegraph and railway freight systems. More and more, too, neutral Switzerland was chosen as the place of meeting for international conferences. The impartial atmosphere of Switzerland seemed to offer the most convenient place of meeting and free discussion. This provoked, it is true, some banter about diplomatic tourist traffic, but there is no question that Switzerland's international standing was raised by her lending Swiss territory for negotiations or for the settlement of European differences, quite apart from the fact " that it is an absolute duty for a neutral state like Switzerland to leave no stone unturned in order to help in the peaceful settlement of international crises," as the Federal Council put it. Thus for instance in 1912, after the Italo-Turkish war about Tripoli, the peace negotiations took place at Lausanne-Ouchy, and in 1913, forty-one members of the German Reichstag met one-hundred-and-sixty-four French deputies and twenty-one senators at Berne for a conference of mutual understanding. The result of the meeting was the inter-parliamentary committee which met at Basle just before the outbreak of the first world war.

It seemed a matter of course that Switzerland should take part in the peace conferences at The Hague. Switzerland signed all the points agreed upon in 1899 with the exception of that dealing with land warfare, since it denied military privileges to a people rising against an invading army. On the other hand the Confederation unanimously adopted the resolutions of the second Hague conference in 1907, at which the position of the neutral state was also discussed.

It was, however, the steady growth of Switzerland's defensive strength which did most to inspire respect for Swiss neutrality both at home and abroad. In 1907 a law was enacted providing for extensive improvements of the army, and in 1912 an army reform came into force which much increased its mobility and striking power. By this reform the strength of the Swiss army was placed at 281,000 men with 200,000 auxiliary troops. A large number of observations by leading military men from various countries testify to the increase of respect for the Swiss army. The Federal Council's consistent policy of armed defence of neutrality was crowned on December 21st, 1912, by a proclamation to the army commanders on the application of neutrality, the first injunction being strictest impartiality. The attitude of neutral Switzerland in case of war was thereby clearly and resolutely defined.

Chapter 15

ARMED NEUTRALITY IN THE FIRST WORLD WAR

The outbreak of the first world war did not find Switzerland unprepared. When a military conflict between the great Powers seemed imminent, the Federal Council, in firm recognition of its responsibility, ordered the mobilization of the whole Swiss army on July 31st, 1914 and took its first military and economic precautions. The main purpose of this obviously defensive measure was to avert an invasion. The Federal Assembly gave the Federal Council plenary powers for the maintenance of national security, and appointed Ulrich Wille General, and Theophil Sprecher von Bernegg Chief of the General Staff. The Council announced to the signatories of the neutrality act of 1815, as well as to the other states, the firm determination of Switzerland "faithful to her century-old tradition, not to depart in any way from the principles of neutrality." This attitude, dictated both by historical development and the actual situation, seemed so obvious that it surprised nobody, whether at home or abroad. Switzerland was most likely the only state at the time from which no ill was expected.

The German invasion of Belgium startled large sections of the population and deeply influenced public opinion, expecially in French Switzerland. More and more the Central Powers seemed to incorporate the idea of pure power and the absolutist, anti-democratic principle, which, it was said, was at profound variance with the principle of liberalism. The greatest European threat to law and democracy came from Germany. The number of Germans in Switzerland was becoming ominous. In intellectual matters, German influence was actually very pronounced, while the German ascendency in economic life was causing great uneasiness. For years, German Switzerland had been following with admiration the rise of Germany in technology, economics and the respect of the world. In the firm security of their own peculiar Alemannic mode of existence, which found expression in their dialects, the German Swiss imagined that they could think and feel with the Germans without sacrificing their own national or surrendering their own cultural ideal. Many deplored the act of violence against Belgium and regret was expressed in the Federal Assembly at the violation of Belgian neutrality, but that by no means prevented them from believing in Germany.

This attitude in French and German Switzerland towards the belligerents was, however, not without its reservations. In any case, with a population of such mixed race as the Confederation, the two camps could not be precisely delimited, whether by geography or by race. Thus conservative protestant groups in French Switzerland sympathized with protestant Germany, while convinced democrats in German Switzerland took the side of the western Powers. Again, German Swiss in trade and industrial circles which had always been in touch with England and America were inclined to their cause. The battle of opinion was envenomed by the stream of foreign lies and propaganda which poured unchecked into the country. A struggle for the soul of the neutrals set in which took on the ugly look of a continuation of the war fought out with pen and ink on Swiss soil. As in every previous European war, the partisans of the various sides came into violent contact in Switzerland, but never had the passions set loose by the strife of opinion run so high. Then prominent intellectuals began to speak, warning their nearest countrymen to take thought and to help to bridge the gulf. The speech of Carl Spitteler, delivered at this time, has become famous. With true independence of spirit, yet without presumption, he defined the Swiss ideal of neutrality with dignity and humaneness, and expressed his compassion with all the belligerents.

At the outbreak of war, the immediate occupation of the frontiers seemed the supreme necessity to all concerned. Within a few days the mobilization of the entire army of 250,000 men was complete. The main body was concentrated at the north-west corner of the country, in order to protect the frontier against both France and Germany. Merciful fate spared the Swiss army the necessity of proving that it was equal to any attempt at a breakthrough by foreign troops. On an average, the élite did about six hundred days' frontier service, the longest for centuries. The long standing-by, the interminable waiting for what might happen, inseparable from a state which was neither peace nor war, made great demands in the endurance and morale of the men. War-like activity can spur the defensive will, while inactivity, often felt as a denial of heroism, in the long run wears men down. As the world war again showed, disaffection appears more readily among the troops who are not under fire. This crisis was fortunately overcome by the Swiss army. In contrast to former European wars there were no grave violations of neutrality. They consisted for the most part of foreign aircraft flying over projecting tongues of land ; occasionally foreign patrols lost their way and strayed over the frontier by mistake.

Switzerland was threatened not only from the military but also from the economic side. It was doubtful whether the little inland state, in the midst of Europe in arms, would not fall victim to famine. For its agricultural produce was insufficient to feed the population and its industry was largely dependent on foreign raw materials. Hence the stoppage of imports of foodstuffs and raw materials could not but become vitally critical in the Confederation. As Switzerland obtained her corn mainly from Russia and overseas, yet had no direct access to the sea, she was dependent on the good will of her neighbours for the continuance of her communication with her foreign food sources.

When the belligerent powers completely blockaded each other, the provision of food and raw material became the supreme and most thorny problem confronting the government. Switzerland was obliged from the outset to face the fact that she could not take her stand on the provisions for neutral trade in international law. In their life and death struggle, the belligerents ceased to respect the principles of international law and paid small heed to Swiss protests. Their only object was to throttle their enemies' trade, to starve them into submission. They would not, therefore, allow the neutrals to re-export imported goods to their neighbours. In order to rescue the national food-supply, Switzerland was obliged to submit to a control of her imports, especially of food and raw materials, which meant a serious infringement of her sovereignty.

If Switzerland was not allowed to starve, the reasons were not entirely humanitarian ; they were utilitarian also. The maintenance of Swiss neutrality seemed desirable not only for military reasons, for the shortening of lines of battle and the internment of sick prisoners of war. Both sides had recourse to the neutral country for the supply of war material and goods for civilian use. The far-reaching industrialisation of Switzerland enabled her to cope with the orders of the belligerents almost in their entirety. If the Powers were to retain this source of supply, it was not enough to provide Switzerland with materials ; her food requirements had also to be covered.

However divided sympathies with the belligerents may have been in Switzerland, the country was unanimous in its desire to help. When the Swiss looks back to what was done at that time, he does so, not with a feeling of complacency in a work of charity, but with profound gratitude to the merciful fate which shielded his country from armed conflict in a flaming ring of warring nations. He has always regarded his humanitarian exertions as a plain fulfilment of duty. He may also indulge in the quiet hope that this active helpfulness of an active neutrality may cancel some portion of the general guilt. Immediately on the outbreak of war, a number of countries entrusted to Switzerland the protection of the interests of their subjects in enemy countries. Since the scope of such activity grew steadily, the Political Department had to create a special service for the representation of foreign interests. A greater burden on the Confederation was the repatriation of foreign civilians, the exchange of sick and disabled soldiers and the internment of invalid prisoners of war. From 1916 till the end of the war, Switzerland accommodated some 68,000 internees. The International Red Cross at Geneva accomplished alone a gargantuan task. Faithful to its tradition of philanthropy, the city of Geneva became the centre of a widespread international assistance. The Committee of the Red Cross employed an army of voluntary workers. Among other things it created the office for the missing and prisoners of war, where lists of the dead and prisoners were drawn up, the missing sought for and their families informed as quickly as possible of their whereabouts and state of health. Nor was the generous helpfulness of Switzerland exhausted by these activities. The Swiss regarded it as their noble privilege to alleviate suffering and devoted themselves to the task with real fervour. Countless philanthropic institutions were created, each with its specific purpose. They assisted the suffering and carried on their work long after the end of the war.

The treaty of Versailles, which was greeted in many places in Switzerland by the ringing of bells, also settled matters which directly affected the Confederation—the shipping on the Rhine, the international convention on the Gotthard railway and the neutrality of northern Savoy. In Art. 435 the treaty Powers recognized an agreement between France and Switzerland abrogating the provisions relating to the neutrality zone of Savoy, Switzerland thus surrendering her right to a military occupation of Upper Savoy. A new generation regarded this point, to which their ancestors had clung so tenaciously, as a relic of the past which had become valueless both from the political and the military point of view. It was a similar notion of neutrality which led Switzerland not to comply with the request by the Austrian Vorarlberg to join the Confederation.

When, towards the end of the war, the ancient idea of a league embracing all nations equally took firmer shape, it awakened an eager echo in Switzerland ; it was assumed that the choice of Geneva as the headquarters of the League of Nations and the International Labour Office had been determined, at any rate in part, by the fact of Swiss neutrality. The publication of the full text of the League of Nations Covenant caused all the greater disappointment. In spite of important objections on principle to the Covenant, Switzerland showed herself willing to co-operate actively in the creation of a lasting world peace. But before she could contemplate joining the League, the question of her neutrality had to be made perfectly clear. No one wished to surrender the fundamental political law, the actual vital principle of the Confederation, which had been maintained for four hundred years. After Switzerland had surrendered her right to the neutrality of Upper Savoy, the Powers, in Art. 435 of the Treaty, recognized Swiss neutrality as an international obligation for the preservation of peace. Switzerland, however, desired an official pronouncement defining more precisely the rights and the nature of Swiss neutrality within the framework of the League of Nations.

That was done in 1920 in the Declaration of London by the League of Nations Council, the Council acknowledging that Switzerland occupied a peculiar position owing to her century-old tradition. It therefore recognized that the permanent neutrality of Switzerland and the guarantee of her territorial integrity, which had been made provisions of international law by the treaties of 1815, were justified in the interests of the general peace and therefore consistent with the League of Nations. The Confederation would be called on neither to participate in military actions, nor to suffer the transit of foreign troops, nor even the preparation of military operations on its territory. It was, however, bound to join in the economic sanctions applied by the League to covenant-breaking nations.

It was only on the basis of the exceptional position thus achieved that the Federal Council felt able to recommend without reserve that the country should join the League. Originally it had intended to make the whole question depend on the entry of the United States, but eventually abandoned that proviso. The opponents of the League wished to remain aloof in order to avoid quitting the ground of absolute law, that is, of total neutrality and entering into what might be at any rate moral dependence. They felt it especially painful that the Federal Council had allowed Swiss neutrality to be confirmed, as if the Swiss principle of state could not exist by its own will and right. The protagonists of the League, for their part, declared that there was no question of sacrificing neutrality on the altar of the League. On the contrary, the international covenant afforded every member the greatest freedom. Neutrality was not the same thing as self-seeking aloofness. Caught up in the post-war mood with its ideal of the brotherhood of nations, they did not believe that the old balance of power policy of the great Powers would ever be resuscitated, to make Switzerland rue the abandonment of her absolute neutrality. On May 16th, 1920, the people voted for entry with 414,830 to 322,937 votes. The majority of the States vote was very meagre—11½ to 10½.

H

Chapter 16

RETURN FROM DIFFERENTIAL TO INTEGRAL NEUTRALITY

Whatever the subsequent opinion of Switzerland's entry into the League of Nations may be, one thing is certain. After the great perils of the war years, the participation in the international peace organization offered the small state of Switzerland the much-desired sense of security which it had so painfully missed in its voluntary isolation. That it was possible to contribute to the international policy of collective security while still preserving and realizing Swiss interests is due primarily to the federal structure of the Swiss state, which in certain aspects represents a miniature League of Nations and therefore has several vital interests in common with it.

From the outset Switzerland defined the peculiarity of her neutral position in the Assembly of the League of Nations with all desirable clarity. She declined on principle to share the responsibility for such actions of the Council as she had no part in, and further, true to her traditional attitude, refused to assume any of the territorial guarantees which the League had stipulated in favour of the victor Powers. Switzerland, however, found herself in a somewhat delicate position when it came to provisions of the Treaty of Versailles the execution of which had to be supervised by the League. On the one hand, Switzerland had not signed the treaty, and hence could legitimately feel that she had no obligations on that score. On the other hand, as a member of the League she was under the obligation of solidarity. In this ambiguous position, which could not but lead to compromises, Switzerland sought to give clear expression to her neutral attitude.

It was also consonant with Swiss neutrality that Switzerland should direct her attention quite particularly to such aims of the League of Nations as were concerned with the development of international relations under international law, and remain aloof from anything connected with the system of sanctions against covenant-breaking states. For the settlement of differences, the League had instituted a complicated arbitration procedure which, however, had no binding character. But Switzerland saw precisely in a binding character the surest guarantee of enduring peace. The Swiss delegation was indefatigable in support of the compulsory settlement of international differences based on a firmly established arbitration procedure. What Switzerland was primarily aiming at was bi-lateral treaties with other states on arbitration and led the way with Poland and Denmark in signing the article dealing with compulsory arbitration.

A characteristic example of the attitude of neutral Switzerland can be seen in her behaviour during the so-called Vilna crisis. In 1920, Polish freebooters occupied the town of Vilna in violation of the armistice with Lithuania. To put an end to the dispute, the Council of the League decided to organize a vote under the protection of international troops. These Belgian, English, and Spanish contingents were to be sent via Switzerland, Austria and Czechoslovakia. Switzerland, however, taking her stand on the Declaration of London, categorically refused free passage to the troops. Thereby she avoided what might have been a dangerous precedent and clearly demonstrated that the League, in any military enterprise, whatever its aims, could not enter Swiss territory.

On the other hand, Switzerland emerged from her reserve in foreign policy when her neighbour, Austria, threatened with financial ruin, required financial help. Yet even here she managed to avoid any international commitment. That Switzerland should also lay aside her reserve when it came to the adoption of Germany into the League is comprehensible if we remember how desirable it was for her to see her most powerful neighbour incorporated in the great international peace organization to which Switzerland herself belonged. Indeed, Switzerland regarded it as one of her prime duties in the League to be the protagonist of its universality. Nor could it be prejudicial to her neutrality if she joined an international agreement such as the Kellogg Pact, which banned war as an instrument of national policy. For the principles of that declaration of peace were identical with the principles represented by Switzerland.

That Switzerland could share without reserve in the philanthropic activities of the League without detriment to her neutrality goes without saying : for instance in the Commission on Hygiene, Intellectual Co-operation, the Drug Traffic, the White Slave Traffic, the repatriation of prisoners of war from Russia and Siberia, the International Labour Office, all kinds of international economic questions and so on. Further, Switzerland supplied the League with a number of prominent experts for the solution of difficult questions, who undertook and carried out their duties not as representatives of Switzerland, but unofficially and quite personally.

After 1930, symptoms of a process of disintegration in the League increased. Its breakdown over the Sino-Japanese crisis of 1930 and the failure of the Disarmament Conference seemed like omens of impending disaster. The more the process of dissolution advanced, the less the small state of Switzerland had to hope from the international organization. Hence Switzerland had to be increasingly careful to keep free of any international involvements, to maintain her impartiality in the coming formation of blocs, and to depend exclusively on her own strength. What that meant was the return from differential to integral neutrality.

This line of development became the more obvious when Hitler's Germany left the Disarmament Conference and the League on October 14th, 1933. Although Switzerland was not directly affected by that step, it meant a new danger if only on account of her geographical situation. She sought to meet it by strengthening the national defences. Relations with Germany were proceeding on not unfriendly lines when they were disturbed, the following year, by a press war, as a result of which the government of the Reich refused to allow the leading Swiss newspapers to enter Germany. Switzerland protested passionately in the name of the freedom of the press and resisted any attempt to expand the interpretation of neutrality. The responsible leader of Swiss foreign policy defended this attitude in an important statement : " The term neutrality is applicable to the State and not to the People. Neutrality is equivalent to the determination not to side with belligerents. The question of individual or even collective sympathies has nothing to do with neutrality." In 1937, Hitler, the Chancellor of the Reich, officially declared that he would respect the neutrality of Switzerland.

It was also urgent for the Swiss Federal Government to maintain friendly relations with the neighbour state of Fascist Italy. At the end of 1924 it concluded an arbitration treaty. Swiss-Italian relations were put to a severe test in the Abyssinian War. The question was whether Switzerland was to join in the sanctions applied to Italy by the League of Nations in 1935. On the one hand, as a member of the League, the Confederation was bound by treaty to take its share in the economic sanctions of the League, on the other, not only reasons of state but a neutral feeling rooted in an old tradition was against unneutral political action against a friendly neighbour. Swiss foreign policy was here confronted with one of its most delicate problems. The representative of Switzerland in the Assembly of the League of Nations stated that Switzerland recognized on principle her obligation to take part in economic and financial sanctions, but that she must abide by her principle of neutrality. In accordance with this view she participated in the embargo on the export of arms, but, in old Swiss fashion, applied it to both belligerents, *i.e.* to Abyssinia also. Switzerland also joined in the refusal of credit and the embargo on the export of war goods, but refused to join in the boycott of Italian goods and the suspension of trade relations.

In 1937, after the abrogation of the sanctions against Italy, the idea slowly gained ground in Switzerland that the collective security of the League of Nations, given its critical condition, could no longer afford sufficient protection to the small state of Switzerland. She was confirmed in this view by statements made by prominent statesmen, among others by Neville Chamberlain, the British Premier. It is obvious that the *anschluss* of Austria to Greater Germany in 1938 precipitated Switzerland's efforts to regain her absolute neutrality. On May 14th, that aim was attained, thanks to the high international standing of Federal Councillor Motta. On that day the Assembly of the League of Nations passed a motion in the following terms : " In consideration of the peculiar situation of Switzerland due to her perpetual neutrality, the League of Nations takes cognizance of the intention of Switzerland not to participate henceforth in any way in the application of sanctions provided for by the Covenant and declares that she shall no longer be called upon to do so."

Thus after eighteen years of riding the ever more perilous high seas of collective security, Switzerland had withdrawn to her old harbour, to the mountain island of absolute neutrality whence, in a position chosen by herself, and relying only on her own strength, she awaited the oncoming tidal wave.

Chapter 17

ABSOLUTE NEUTRALITY IN THE SECOND WORLD WAR

The outbreak of the second world war found Switzerland in a far better position, military, economic and moral, than the first. For some years before, the Confederation had observed with growing dismay that no country in the world really took collective security seriously, and therefore that no country was going to risk any essential reduction of its armaments. The lamentable course of the Disarmaments Conference seemed to mean that the world was again to be ruled by the principle that might is right, and not by written guarantees. As Switzerland's neighbours to north and south proceeded to transform themselves into huge military camps governed by the spirit of military aggression, the Swiss had to face the bitter truth that the strengthening of the national defences was one of the supreme duties of the state. The Bund bought arms and munitions ; in 1935 the period of military training was lengthened by general consent, while new army regulations were introduced in 1938. Two years previously the Swiss nation had already subscribed a national defence loan of 322 m. Swfr., a clear sign of its determination to defend the country. All these were enormous sacrifices, considering the size of the country and the critical times it was passing through. These plebiscites were accepted all over the country as the expression of an unconditional will to be prepared, which was shared by all parties, including the Social Democrats.

Economic and military preparation went hand in hand. The experience gained in the first world war made it abundantly clear that a country poor in raw materials and surrounded by belligerents would suffer acutely from isolation. State storehouses and private storerooms were filled, and if Switzerland was able to hold out to the end of the war, that was largely due to such measures. In the course of a stirring speech held after the rape of Austria, the head of the Department of National Economy said : " The world at large must realize that whoever respects us and leaves us in peace is our friend. But whoever is guilty of any attack on our independence and political integrity must expect war. We Swiss are not going begging."

Meanwhile, the assertion of the Swiss way of life became firmer as the pan-German doctrine of National Socialism became more aggressive. Fresh thought was given to the Swiss constitution, which had been taken for granted far too long, and its basic principles were re-examined. The country took serious stock of itself. It turned to its history to discover the bond between past and present, and sources of fresh energy for the future. The Swiss form of democracy was recognized as a fusion of Swiss liberties with the present-day rational conception of freedom, and the line of demarcation drawn between Swiss democracy, as an organic and popular growth, and other continental democracies. Federalism, which unites on an equal footing member states differing in culture and size, thus providing of itself the solution of the minorities problem, was seen to be the inherent form of the Swiss nation as founded by the will of the people—diversity in unity. When it transpired that, in German training regulations, Switzerland was simply regarded as part of the Reich, and incorporated in the Reich on official maps, the Confederation was roused to double its resistance to such arrogant assumptions.

When war at last broke out, the General was elected by the Federal Assembly with few dissentient voices. It seemed like an open rejection of the nature of German militarism that Henri Guisan, a native of the canton of Vaud, should be put in command of the Swiss armed forces by 204 votes out of 229. Throughout the period of mobilization, General Guisan retained the affection of all parts of the country and all classes of the people. The Federal Assembly proclaimed the firm will of the Confederation " to preserve its neutrality in all circumstances and with regard to all Powers." At the end of August, 1939, and in almost the same terms as in 1914, the Federal Council issued a proclamation of its neutrality to the Powers and gave the order to mobilize, which was followed only two days later by the order for general national service. The country was determined not to be drawn into any conflict.

At the outbreak of war, 400,000 men were under arms. In the course of time this number was increased to 850,000 by the Auxiliary Forces and the Local Guards. The number mobilized never dropped below 100,000, an impressive figure in proportion to the total population of only four millions. Other countries began to realize that Switzerland would throw all her resources into the struggle against any power which attacked her. At the beginning of the war, the military situation resembled that of 1914. Switzerland was surrounded by belligerents or countries not yet involved in the war. To meet this situation, the northern and eastern frontiers were strongly manned, while the defence of the south and west was relatively weak. The whole outlook, however, was radically changed by the fall of France—which meant the internment of some 50,000 Polish and French troops which had been swept over the Swiss frontiers—and when Italy entered the war. Switzerland was now completely encircled by a single military power, the Axis. The anxious question arose as to what resources the Confederation could command in resistance to the huge armies of tanks mowing down all artificial barriers, the unprecedented number of fighter planes put into action by the Axis powers, the paratroops and the air-borne forces. The civilian population began to leave the most exposed centres for the interior of the country, though there was neither panic nor disorder.

Within a short time the General, abandoning traditional notions of national defence, had revolutionized the entire national defence scheme. He concentrated the main body of the armed forces in the interior of the country in order to create a citadel of Swiss independence in the Alps, temporarily abandoning the frontiers, till then regarded as the bulwarks of the country, and the plains. The term " réduit " is taken from the science of fortification and means a fortress constructed inside another, with the object of prolonging the defence of the main fortress and enabling its defenders to drive the aggressor out. The plan was based on the realization that, in a military struggle against a much superior enemy, part of the country would have to be sacrificed temporarily if the whole was to be saved in the end. That was the reason for the relatively weak defence of the frontiers and the concentrated defence of the interior of the country in the *réduit national*. This idea of the *réduit*, though it was never put to the test, was a comfort to many whose hearts failed them at the most critical moment. Not until the defeated German armies were pursued back into their own country, and the convulsions of the last desperate struggle had set in, did the Swiss forces leave the *réduit* to re-man the frontiers against possible intruders.

Switzerland had more than once been on the point of being invaded by German troops concentrated for the purpose. There is no possible doubt that the " hedgehog " had been marked down long before by the German High Command for inclusion in the military and economic ramifications of their plans for world conquest. Why the plan was ultimately abandoned cannot be said with certainty. The Führer may not have thought it worth while to use the large forces which would have been necessary against a small country with few raw materials. He may have disliked the idea of having those forces kept out of the general action for any length of time. Further, the Gotthard line, by which coal could be transported to his Axis partner, was so useful to him that the destruction of the Gotthard tunnel—it was mined by the Swiss and would have been irrevocably blown up in the case of attack—would have meant too serious a loss. After the landing of the British and American armies in France and North Africa, Germany was fully occupied with her own defence and could not take on another enemy, however small. Thus the neutrality of Switzerland was preserved throughout the war. It was violated from the air many times, at first mainly by German fighter planes, later by the Americans. Considerable damage was done by bombs, the most severe being that caused at Schaffhouse in 1944, when forty people were killed. Switzerland, too, became familiar with the blackout and the howl of the sirens.

As in the first world war, Switzerland's struggle for economic survival was extremely hard. Every effort was made to keep the country free of the blockade and counter-blockade of the belligerents and of their economic control. Threatened with strangulation by the Axis powers, she had to supply them with foodstuffs, manufactured goods and munitions, yet, even at moments of extreme hardship, she never wavered in her neutral principle, laid down in international law, of the equal treatment of all belligerents, and was able to export war material to allied countries through German-occupied territory in spite of the growing shortage of means of transport. It was only by services of this kind rendered to both sides that she was able to obtain the raw material necessary to keep her industry going at all and to overcome critical changes in the economic situation. The exchange of goods with other countries was regulated by trade agreements of increasing difficulty, but Switzerland was never called upon for political concessions or the forced export of labour. The end of the war was to show that the behaviour of Switzerland, approved by both sides and fully consonant with the provisions of international law, was of advantage not only to herself, but to Europe as a whole. After the conclusion of peace, she was able to place her intact economic potential without delay at the services of the urgent necessities of European recovery.

In order to hold out on the economic side, the Swiss had to find fresh sources of food supply within their own country. The trend of agricultural production had to be diverted entirely from export and concentrated on crops and livestock for home consumption. Under the systematic guidance of the Agricultural Commission, grassland was ploughed up, forests were cleared, pastures drained and their productivity increased. A saying was current at the time that the Swiss must kneel in the furrow if they were not to kneel to a foreign master. Every man who could be spared from the army was drafted into land work. By thus diverting its whole production to home consumption, Swiss agriculture was able to feed an industrial population. As in the belligerent countries, all food was strictly rationed.

In the first world war there had been a deep gulf between the French- and German-speaking parts of the country, but in the second they were as one in their resistance to the racial delusions and power politics entering the country from alien sources, whatever their origin. The Swiss maintained their federalism, supported by their faith in the individual destiny of the part within the whole and the realization of the profound significance of a federal organization of law. It was the manifold variety of the different ways of life in the Confederation which had made the Swiss aware of the great values of the individual. Switzerland had no desire to reduce her varied

energies to a common denominator; her task was to unite
them creatively in the consciousness of the Confederation
as a whole. The spiritual and cultural relations between
Alemanic Switzerland and her neighbour Germany, till
then so close, began to slacken. The passionately democratic Ticino allowed its connection with Fascist Italy to
cool, while French Switzerland turned its back on the
Vichy régime in France. This cultural independence was
not set up as a permanent ideal, but was throughout a
temporary and emergency solution.

National Socialism did everything in its power to pro-
pagate its ideas in Switzerland in preparation for the
anschluss. There were organizations which carried on
prohibited propaganda in secret ; people posing as
officials of the German consulates listed Swiss citizens
according to their political ideas, spies were put on the
track of military and economic secrets. The Swiss are a
hard-headed race, and National Socialism found but few
adherents in its efforts to organize treason. Dazzled by
the spurious brilliance of the new German ideals, or misled
by the promise of payment, not more than a handful of
Swiss were decoyed into serving the enemy and preparing
acts of sabotage. Seventeen traitors were shot by order
of the courts martial, and fourteen condemned to death
in absentia. But there was never a dangerous fifth column
in Switzerland such as had prepared the way for Hitler
in every country he overran. All parties were united in
their abhorrence of the foreign doctrines and openly
asserted their faith in the ideals of their own country. Its
liberties seemed the stoutest shield and buckler against
totalitarianism of any kind or origin. The party truce
found visible expression in the entrance of the Social
Democrats into the Federal Council, the Swiss executive.
Meanwhile, the country as a whole was paying far more
serious attention to social reform, and promoting the
development of the welfare state in the Confederation. In

this way a constructive collaboration grew up among the parties. This united front within the country was its most effective means of defence. For, as historical experience has shown, Switzerland has never succumbed to foreign aggression except when her defences were paralysed by internal discord or when the enemy had found accomplices in treachery in the country itself.

To prevent any doubts arising at home or abroad as to the political attitude of the government and military leaders, a declaration was issued in 1940 in the following terms : " Should news be spread by wireless, leaflets or other means casting doubt on the determination of the Federal Council or the General Staff to defend the country, such news is to be regarded as a fabrication of the enemy. Our country will resist aggression with all the means in its power and to the bitter end." In spite of this official stiffening of the spirit of resistance, not a few Swiss succumbed soon afterwards to the general shock of Hitler's victories. In that unhappy summer of 1940, the whole situation seemed desperate. France, which had been looked to for support in the case of a German attack, was crushed from without and eaten away from within by rapid deterioration, and laid down her arms. Holland, Belgium, Luxemburg and Denmark were overrun, Italy entered the war on the side of her Axis partner and Russia was allied with Germany. England alone carried on the struggle, but withdrew to her island, remote and inaccessible to Switzerland. Defeatist voices were already raised in public by prominent men, advising a political and economic readjustment. Evil rumours spread through the country, exacerbating the war of nerves and disheartening the people. But the violent reaction they provoked bears fine witness to the steadiness and soundness of popular feeling in Switzerland, which also found a support in the consistently firm attitude of the General. At the end of July he summoned a meeting of the higher army officers on the Rütli " in order that all may hear the mysterious call which rises from this place." In an inspiring speech he drove home to his hearers the necessity for unflinching resistance. The speech sounded like Switzerland's answer to the presumptuous demands of the world conquerors. Defeatism practically disappeared as a mass phenomenon. In 1942 the Federal Council made " any publicity tending to sacrifice the national neutrality " a punishable offence.

It was with the utmost reluctance, and only in face of the huge German armed forces, that the Swiss people submitted to certain restrictions of their liberties. While it is natural, in time of crisis, for a democracy to depute its powers to a small body capable of rapid action, it is nevertheless dangerous to forfeit those liberties for any length of time. How double-edged a defensive weapon of the kind may be was illustrated by the introduction of the press censorship. Its object was to prevent any provocation of the German apostles of force by heedless attacks in the press. But the danger was that the suppression of news of German action might lull the vigilant spirit of resistance in Switzerland. And indeed, this restriction of the liberty of the press and the steps taken by the censorship roused repeated and passionate controversy. In spite of the censorship, the press of all political parties published all the essential news, for the people as a whole realized that in a democracy like Switzerland, foreign policy could not be withheld from public discussion, and claimed the right, even as a neutral country, to form an independent opinion on world events.

The suppression of the Communist Party, which had taken place before the war, and that of the Fascist fronts, met with practically unanimous approval. Political parties which counted in any way on foreign help to obtain power at a time when the national existence was at stake seemed to stand convicted of moral treason. In order to protect its liberties, even the democratic and neutral state had to have recourse to repressive measures.

Public opinion in Switzerland, however, was divided on the question of the exercise of the right of asylum. The stream of refugees into the country which had already set in in 1933 now swelled to unprecedented proportions. Left to themselves, the Swiss people would have swept away all frontier barriers and taken in all the thousands who were striving to save their lives, if nothing else, from the fury of their persecutors. But the government was soon warning the people of the dangers of the " overcrowded boat," and stressing the inexorable limits set to the grant of asylum. In spite of all, Switzerland, in the darkest days and in the teeth of the German rulers, gave asylum to over 100,000 refugees.

In a general way the Confederation regarded it as a duty and a neutral privilege to alleviate the sufferings of war so far as lay in its power and subject to the provisions of international law. In addition to all the work done by a large number of private charities, in addition to that of the Red Cross and its auxiliary organizations, mention should be made of the services rendered to the belligerents by the representation of foreign interests in enemy territory. Here very thorny tasks fell to Switzerland's lot. The work of charity was crowned by the creation of the Swiss National Fund for the Relief of War Victims, which, by 1948, had reached a total of 250 m. Swfr. True to the ancient principles of neutrality, help was given to nationals of all the belligerent countries : France, Italy, Austria, Germany, Belgium, Holland, Luxemburg, Norway, England, Finland, Poland, Czechoslovakia, Hungary, Yugoslavia, Albania, Greece, Roumania, Bulgaria. Food, clothing, shoes, medicines, tools, building materials, agricultural equipment and seeds were distributed, huts built for emergency housing and workshops, surgical, orthopaedic and technical missions were organized, while

Swiss hospitals took in tens of thousands of children threatened with, and adults suffering from, tuberculosis, as well as other disabled persons.

When at last the noise of arms died down in 1945, a sigh of relief ran through the whole country. Switzerland could say that she had kept to the last letter the promise she had given in her declaration of neutrality in 1939. The end of the war was hailed as the awakening from a nightmare whose stifling pressure she had felt for years. She could at last issue from her enforced isolation and gradually resume her natural and close relations with the free nations. The resumption of relations with Russia, interrupted since 1921, was in keeping with the neutral principle of equality in the treatment of all countries, while taking into account the redistribution of power. Switzerland was ready to work sincerely for the new community of nations which was to arise from a world in travail, for it was hoped that the new world order would not consist in the subjection of the world by a few great powers, with the small nations forced to abandon their right of self-determination and their own way of life. It was the realization of the high function of neutrality which united the government and the people in their determination never to surrender the principle of Swiss independence, which had stood the test for centuries, but only to enter the new security organization of UNO if their permanent neutrality could be preserved.

Chapter 18

HOSTILE CRITICISMS OF NEUTRALITY

This historical survey clearly shows how the principle of neutrality in foreign relations has grown by natural necessity out of the national existence of the Confederation, its geographical situation, its federal structure, its position as a minor state, its religious cleavage, its multi-racial character and its democratic organization. These constants of Swiss life are all interrelated and inter-dependent. With them, neutrality forms one organic whole, no element of which can be torn out without grievous harm to the rest. It is the axiom of Swiss sovereignty which has borne the test of centuries of foreign relations. For the experience of Swiss history yields one perfectly unambiguous result—without neutrality, no national sovereignty. But without neutrality also, no Swiss freedom, which must be taken to cover the manifold institutions of liberty which are regarded by the world as being of the very essence of Swiss policy. Only under the shield of neutrality could they thrive and bloom. It was only the subjection of foreign to home policy which permitted Switzerland to give permanence to her free institutions. In the same way, in England it was the long peace due to her insular position which enabled her free institutions to develop, a blessing which rarely falls to the lot of the great power. For the great power generally makes its home policy the handmaid of its foreign policy, and often, to assert its power, must order its internal organization to meet the needs of foreign policy.

The insight into the high function of neutrality as the foundation on which the Swiss body politic rests should be sufficient to silence any doubts as to the worth or worth-lessness of the Swiss principle in foreign relations. Yet questions born of those doubts are constantly and passionately raised, and neutrality is violently attacked from within by the Swiss themselves. Even in the 19th century, in the infancy of the policy, members of one religious party advocated the surrender of neutrality in order that they might go to the help of their brothers in the faith abroad. In Zurich, the head of the clergy preached on the text in Revelations : " So then because thou art lukewarm, and neither cold nor hot, I will spue thee out of my mouth." And a broadside of the period poured scorn on the " mad folly of this shameful and horrible neutrality. The middle or neutral way is not that of the good Christian, but the most wretched of all." In the middle of the 19th century, prominent politicians demanded that Switzerland should help neighbour peoples struggling for their freedom, raising the slogan of the solidarity of the people. This idea of Switzerland's liberating mission, actually mooted in the central governing body of the Confederation, is an hallucination which carried away enthusiastic spirits at the time, and has infected the usually somewhat unimaginative and rationally minded Swiss at other times too. We have only to think of the high Helvetic mood which reigned at the foundation of the League of Nations. In the recent Spanish civil war, and again in the present war, Switzerland has been called on to take sides in the conflict of principle between two opposing political systems.

All these demands for an occasional surrender of Swiss neutrality in favour of some high human ideal show a complete lack of understanding for the vital conditions of Swiss life, and further testify to the absence of a nice appreciation of the power ratio in Europe. The political wisdom of official Switzerland has always clung to traditional neutrality in the teeth of such dubious tendencies, even when they made themselves felt in great force. Today the proposals for an organization of international security after the present war once more raises the question of the justification of a neutral Switzerland in a Europe united against all law and peace breakers. But even in League of Nations circles it is recognized that Switzerland must retain the right of making no kind of sacrifice of her neutrality until the new system of collective security has proved itself to be a really super-national institution of law. At present it certainly does not look if a condition could be arrived at in anything like the near future which could make even a differential neutrality such as existed between 1920 and 1938 a question of practical politics.

Swiss neutrality has also, or even mainly, been called in question outside of the country. We can understand that every belligerent should try to persuade Switzerland to take sides. The moral and legal invective, however, only gained strength at the beginning of last century during the German wars of liberation, as has been shown above. From the standpoint of a European legal order mainly directed by Prussia and Austria, Swiss neutrality was the object of severe criticism, the polemical intentions of which were not difficult to discern. Space forbids the quotation of more than a few of the voices then raised in chorus, but it was said, for instance that " no belligerent power should suffer the egoism which looks on, furtively spying out its own advantage," for that meant graver dangers than open violence. In Germany it was noted with satisfaction that the idea of neutrality, condemned as weakness, could be rendered by no native word. Finally, neutrality was seen to be unlawful since it stood in contradiction to the natural law of nations. Switzerland was asked whether she would not abandon her unnatural neutrality and return to the Germanic Central European state.

The Confederation resisted these blandishments, just as it resisted the torrent of propagandist literature which poured over the country in 1914–1918. At that time Swiss neutrality stood low in the world's esteem, for it will always be difficult to make other countries realize the intrinsic nature of the Swiss attitude in foreign relations. For a country fighting desperately for its life in the sincere belief that it is staking all for the highest aims of humanity, the quietude, the aloofness, the apparent insensitiveness of a third party always awakes suspicion and breeds contempt. Should the neutrals be better off than the belligerents, they are soon accused of exploiting their neutrality for purposes of economic welfare, a reproach which has been unjustly brought against Switzerland in every European war for more than two hundred years.

The Swiss writer, Heinrich Federer has taken the state of mind just described as the subject of one of his most touching stories : *Unser Herrgott und die Schweizer.* Wounded soldiers of all nations involved in the international struggle call the Swiss to account for themselves before the throne of God. " Neutral—what does that mean ? " cries a bleeding sergeant. " Day is not neutral, nor is night. Nothing wholesome or hearty on earth is neutral ; only the bat is neutral. And the Swiss is terribly like a bat, fluttering about between light and dark, neither fish nor bird—just neutral. Lord God, Thou hast said Thyself in St. John or St. Luke that neutrality is a grievous sin. Punish it then ! " God then listens to the bungling defence of the Swiss and exhorts him to humility and to active philanthropy. Then, turning to the soldiers, He takes up the defence of Swiss neutrality : " Who would be so foolish as to drag into the general filth and strife this tiny spot of earth where men may still hold out in fellowship hands not stained with blood ? Leave the Swiss alone. And believe Me, it does not only take courage to be the storm : it takes courage to be the island in the storm."

After the first world war, the onslaughts on Swiss neutrality died down, only to set in again in the 1930's with unprecedented force. In a pseudo-scientific treatise incorporating the dawning doctrine of race and the totalitarian ideal of the state, the neutrality of Switzerland was viciously distorted and slandered and branded as a weakness of will, as a moral defect, as senility, as disease. Neutrality, it was said, was the symptom of a European sickness, the negation of all politics, was sterility, rootlessness, scepticism, in fact the refusal of a destiny (Christoph Steding : *Das Reich und die Krankheit der europäischen Kultur ;* Hamburg, 1938). A famous international lawyer from the opposing camp of partisans of the League of Nations proclaimed the decay of the idea of neutrality as a scientific fact. The author claims to have proved : " que la neutralité apparaît aujourd'hui comme un véritable anachronisme ; n'étant plus en harmonie avec l'état du droit des gens ni avec les nécessités économiques et les aspirations des peuples, elle est irrémédiablement condamnée comme institution ; elle est destinée à disparaître " (Nicolas Politis : *La Neutralité et la Paix ;* Paris, 1935). And only recently a widely read book by an English writer expressed the view : " Neutrality is finished as a political concept," that the minor states of Europe " must henceforth surrender their sovereign rights of neutrality " (Julian Huxley : *Democracy Marches ;* New York, 1941). The most recent criticism, and the anti-neutral trend of the day, are based on the new conception of peace among the victor powers, but reveal other undertones, such as the idea of the solidarity of Western Europe.

In Switzerland these calumnies and prophecies of woe are taken quite coolly, and the native equanimity remains unshaken. Either they are disproved by present political conditions, or they stand self-condemned by their own tendentiousness. That Swiss neutrality is no bed of roses on which the Swiss, heedless of the way of the world, lose the habit of effort is proved by their labours in the military and economic spheres. And that neutrality alone is no guarantee against attack from the outside, but demands extreme vigilance from every citizen, has been shown by the most recent past. The ridiculous assumption that neutrality is the necessary attribute of an ageing people is disproved precisely by the early history of Prussia-Brandenburg. Further, the assertion that Europe granted Switzerland her neutrality, and can therefore take it back again, is countered by the Swiss with the historical fact that their neutrality is no charitable gift of the great Powers, but was—though not arbitrarily—chosen and desired by them within definite laws dictated by the necessities of their political existence. It is just because they have declared their neutrality permanent, and therefore do not change their views on foreign affairs in the vicissitudes of international relations, that they are proof against the charge of time-serving. The Swiss bear the heavy burden of their armed neutrality without any intention of exploiting changed political constellations for the acquisition of power, in sharp contrast to the occasional neutrals or "non-belligerents." As long as there is no really super-national court of arbitration in international relations, the neutral Swiss has every right to decline to shed his blood in the interests of a system of great Powers.

The misgivings that arise at home, however, are far more serious and dangerous than foreign invective. For is not neutrality an inglorious and paltry ideal at a time which demands the supreme sacrifice from every man? What ardour or energy can it inspire? Is it not too cool for hot-blooded youth, too many-facetted for an age which loves clear-cut issues? What enthusiasm can be felt for an attitude which aims at a general insurance against danger ? Is this aloofness not a bare betrayal of what others are giving their lives for ? There is real spiritual distress when a man's general outlook on life is incompatible with the neutral attitude required of him, and when, as a human being, he is at odds with himself as a citizen. Does neutrality not lead to a deadening of moral feeling, does it not, when consistently maintained, end in the abominable condition of a resigned and cowardly indifference ? Or does it not make Pharisees of men because, not being in the heat and tumult of the battle, they imagine they are above it ?

Clear definitions soon dispel confusions of this kind. Neutrality is a principle of foreign policy, not of ethics. It presents a programme of foreign relations, not a moral ideal. For the Swiss it is a method of political diplomacy, not the goal of their being as a nation. Switzerland is not there for neutrality, but neutrality for Switzerland. In neutrality, the Swiss see a product of the reason of state which aims at the welfare of the state and of the community of the people it embraces, but not a fundamental spiritual attitude. That is, the Swiss regard their neutrality solely as an affair of the state and not of the private individual. Their neutrality is the fruit of practical experience, not of theoretical speculation, of cool rationalism, not of elemental instinct. In the moral domain the Swiss knows no neutrality. He has to decide between good and evil, right and wrong. Any man refusing to take sides in that conflict and striving to achieve a so-called neutral attitude would prove himself guilty of a lack of logical discrimination, and still more, of a strange moral callousness.

Chapter 19

SUPER-NATIONAL SIGNIFICANCE OF SWISS NEUTRALITY

The Swiss freely admit that they regard neutrality as an instrument of national egoism, as a necessity of state forced upon them by their situation. The same might be said of any reasonable principle of foreign policy. In the present grave anxiety for the life and the future of their native country, the Swiss have the right to regard neutrality in the first place as a mere means of self-preservation, of the preservation of their political independence and national character, without being obliged to justify, let alone extenuate, that axiom by works of philanthropy. In a world which has failed to put super-national law into action and knows no super-national means of keeping the law and preserving peace, the Swiss may have no qualms in refusing to wage war in the interests of a so-called " collective security." It must, however, be said at once and most emphatically that neutrality properly understood and practised expresses the moral convictions of the Swiss and goes far beyond national egoism. The ideal nature of Swiss neutrality derives from its utilitarian character. In the long run the Swiss would be uneasy if they had to live solely for the sake of national selfishness, if they had to deny their traditional humanitarian aims. They regard it as providential that the idea of Switzerland should be so closely akin to the idea of humanitarianism. They may be citizens of the world, not in the sense of a watery cosmopolitanism but in the good and positive sense, and yet be a good Swiss. Indeed, it is just in order that he may be active for the whole of mankind that the Swiss must remain true to himself. To be truly Swiss does not exclude the sense of humanity as a whole, but fosters it or even requires it, for the crampedness of the Confederation demands as a compensation some super-national breadth. To be Swiss only is to be un-Swiss. But it is only as a sovereign state that Switzerland can fulfil her tasks of humane neutrality. Thus the utilitarian instrument of neutrality may serve for the realization of ethical aims.

In this way, Switzerland can turn the neutrality imposed upon her by fate into a creative and living thing, may inspire it with a new and higher significance. Neutrality is then no longer a cold " No " of repudiation towards the outside world, but a warm "Yes" of conviction and the desire to help. We might briefly refer here to the services of the International Red Cross which itself grew out of the permanent neutrality of Switzerland and is based on it, for instance, the care of prisoners of war and civil internees, the transmission of food-parcels and news, and the assistance to distressed civilian populations. In a world at war, the Swiss feel that the right and fitting expression of their own peculiar character and culture is a philanthropy extended equally to all the innocent victims of the upheaval. Nor do they speak of such things in self-glorification, but in order to show how neutrality may take on a deeper meaning. For they know that they are merely paying a small part of their debt of gratitude to the fate which has granted peace to their homeland. It is Switzerland's privilege to be able to help ; by exercising it and thus professing their humanitarian ideals, the Swiss liberate themselves from the mental burden which all neutrals must bear. Thus a wide field is open to eager helpfulness ; for once neutrality knows no limitations. In addition to private welfare, particularly that of the Swiss Red Cross with its child welfare work and other forms of assistance, the state as a whole is active in the service of the belligerents. Among other things the taking charge of foreign interests, *i.e.* the interests of the belligerents, often lays very onerous duties on the Confederation, such as the exchange of diplomatic staffs, and of civilians and disabled soldiers, the visiting of civilian concentration camps and the inspection of prisoner of war camps, the payment of allowances to civilians who have remained in the enemy country, and the formation of mixed medical missions. Then come hospital care for sick combatants, the housing and support of civilian refugees, the repatriation of foreign labourers who have crossed the frontier and the financial support of the work of the International Red Cross and the Swiss Red Cross.

The noblest heritage of neutrality certainly lies in the right of asylum. To offer sanctuary to political fugitives is a right every state possesses, but Switzerland has exercised it at all times with notable generosity, and has become the favourite country of asylum. Public opinion, of late years, has shown how ready she is to carry on that noble tradition within the provisions of international law. The consciousness of the obligation to this part of the past is so deeply rooted in the national mind, and is so much a part of Swiss life, that it can only perish with Switzerland herself. What Switzerland can do in this direction is proved by many a page of her history. We can only wonder at the sacrifices that were made, simply and without a word, without consideration of the state of the national food supply, of political troubles at home and abroad and without a thought of the possible cultural enrichment the exiles might bring, but purely " for the sake of conscience and the Divine compassion," because the fugitives too were " true members and guests of Our Lord Jesus Christ." There were cantons at the end of the 17th century which devoted up to one fifth of all public revenues to the support of refugees from persecution, and imposed the refugee tax under threat of punishment, not to speak of the enormous amount of private charity. A surrender of the principle of asylum would be a self-inflicted wound on the national honour from which the Confederation could hardly recover. Any betrayal of an ideal brings its own revenge with it. The task of Christian brotherhood is a matter of course for the Swiss ; they must not even admit that it could be questioned. Their integral neutrality pledges them to integral humanity.

It is also in order to give a more active meaning to her neutrality that Switzerland feels bound, by her position in the midst of the warring nations, to strive with unremitting self-denial to promote reconciliation by helping to prepare the atmosphere for understanding, since without co-operation there can be no future. This will indeed be one of the greatest and most urgent tasks of the post-war period. Whatever the order of international community may be, it may be confidently predicted that the new peace organization, if it is to endure, will have to be founded on understanding and reconciliation between the free nations of Europe. How glad Europe will be, during the formative period of the future society of states, of any bridge that has not been destroyed, of any bond that has not been broken. It is an easy thing to break off relations, a difficult one to restore them. If the Swiss are to be capable of this post-war achievement, they must not suffer any modification of their inherited standards, must carry over into the post-war period their innate sense of reality and true greatness. They have no fear of drifting into characterlessness if they collaborate in the solution of these international problems. Their own national character is too pronounced, they are too deeply rooted in the native soil. They are presumptuous enough to believe that, though a small country, they can render these services to the belligerents, for they still cannot bring themselves to believe that the worth of a people depends on the number of its guns and soldiers ; it depends on the principles that people embodies and actively practises. In the Confederation, those principles lie in the domain of universal morality ; it is that which gives Swiss neutrality its nobility and its right to survive.

Chapter 20

WHAT IS A NEUTRAL OUTLOOK?

In order, however, to be useful to a world rent with suffering and to help to solve the problems of the future, the Swiss mean to maintain a neutral attitude which is worthy of the name. That does not mean in any way neutrality of conviction, for that is pusillanimity. The Swiss cannot feel that the meaning of neutrality is exhausted by guarding the frontiers and holding their tongues. The human being will always take up his stand at some point, and by his very nature he must take sides—he must hate or love. To take a man's sympathies amiss is to misunderstand the true condition of man. The Confederation is of one mind that there is freedom of conscience even in the sphere of foreign policy. Further, it holds that the obligations of neutrality by no means include the regimentation of public opinion. Their scope cannot be extended to cover the attitude of the press. To put such an extensive construction on neutrality is not Swiss, and finds no foothold in international law. In 1938, Federal Councillor Motta explicitly stated : " We reject the doctrine which attempts to confound the neutrality of the state with the neutrality of the individual ; on principle, only the state is neutral, and will steadfastly remain so. The citizen remains free in his views and judgment. Dispassionate discussion is always allowed to him. We require of him a self-imposed discipline in the way he expresses his views." The theory that the state alone is neutral, but that the subject is not bound by any obligation of international law, and that therefore no violation of neutrality in contravention of international law can be committed by a private person, is universally held in Switzerland. The scope of neutrality has certainly expanded. As war penetrates ever more deeply into the life of the nations, the range of neutrality also expands. But that implies no encroachment on the constitutional principle of the freedom of personal opinion. That point has been made fully clear by discussions in parliament and the public. For it is just in a federal state, of mixed race and language, that discussions of events tend to become most lively.

On the other hand, the subject of the neutral state can be required to put no unnecessary obstacles in the way of its foreign policy. He should remain aloof from the fierce struggle of parties, should fight against feeling in the place of thinking, avoid summary judgments and sympathize with self-control. The Swiss will more readily be temperate in the political struggle since he has proved capable of temperance in the religious struggle. It will certainly be objected that the present conflict is a conflict of ideas. But have the great European conflicts ever been anything else? The struggle for the soul of the neutrals has always been carried on with ideal aims.

No one will be so infatuated as to imagine that because he has had no share in the war he can discern and define all the forces working behind the contending nations. It took long and arduous research before the causes of the first world war were so far cleared up that the dense network of real and apparent causes could be even partially disentangled. Even now, when records have been made accessible and the memoirs of the leading men published, the question of war-guilt can only be approached with the utmost caution, for it is impossible to plumb all the historical depths of that great crisis. For the state and the power of the state are things, as the historian must always remind the moralist, in whose growth and activity free moral choice, the necessity of facing the consequences of that choice, and pure, elemental compulsion are generally so interwoven that no earthly judge will be able to pronounce just judgment with a plain ' good ' or ' evil.'

And there is another point. The Swiss are typically men of a small country. They can, of course, reach an intellectual understanding of life in the great state. But it is more difficult for them, with the long history as a minor and neutral state, to *imagine* life and feeling in a great empire, and assess at its true value that unfathomable compound of pride and self-dedication which usually inspires the leaders of great nations in face of the responsibility they assume for millions and millions of men. Since restraint in judgment and dispassionate reflection seem imperative in private, they are infinitely more so in public.

The tasks laid upon Switzerland seem all the heavier when we consider the size of the country. And are we to believe that neutrality is doomed ? On the contrary, the Swiss believe it to be a living thing, capable of vital growth of a momentous kind. But if past experience is to contribute to a vigorous future, the significance of Switzerland and her neutrality must not occupy in our thoughts a place too nicely proportionate to her geographical bounds.

Chapter 21

SWISS NEUTRALITY AND EUROPEAN UNION

It has become something of a commonplace that Switzerland is the most international country in the world. Or again, Switzerland is praised as being the most European nation in that ancient continent. What do sayings of the kind really mean? Firstly, that Switzerland lies in the heart of Europe, that four great rivers rise there, and that this is the point in Europe where important cultures meet and mingle. Further, that she has at all times been the centre of exchange of spiritual and material goods. All these things have broadened her horizon and deepened her insight into international relations. Moreover, Switzerland unites representatives of three ancient European cultures on an absolutely equal footing and officially recognizes four European languages. For those reasons, and in virtue of her federal structure, she is a Europe in miniature.

A country bound to the outside world by such manifold ties, and itself readily receptive to foreign influences, must at all times be aware of its involvement in the fate of the world as a whole. It is for that reason that Switzerland takes the keenest interest in any movement which aims at world or European organization. It is not by chance that the head offices of so many international unions are to be found at Berne, that the seat of the first supranational association, the League of Nations, was at Geneva, and that after the second world war Winston Churchill proclaimed his idea of a federation of the western nations at Zurich. All these things might lead us to believe that Switzerland would eagerly associate herself with any movement towards an international organization. Yet the fact remains that she plays no leading part in the political union of Europe. Of the five main organizations which have been created in the last few years with the object of world consolidation, Switzerland has joined only two, nor is she represented on the Council of Europe, the most active step taken towards European federation.

This apparent contradiction needs some explanation. The chief factor which prevents her from joining any European or world alliance is her ancient and traditional status of permanent and absolute neutrality. The Swiss of today still understands by neutrality the principles of self-defence, political independence and the national way of life, non-intervention in any system of alliances, the duty of mediation in disputes between the great powers and help in settling them. To the Swiss, the policy of neutrality does not mean moral indifference or political apathy, but a considered standpoint and a general readiness to help, a policy of wisdom, patience, fortitude and peace. This Swiss policy has already been of value to European recovery, yet is constantly misjudged in Europe. In Switzerland itself, where due value is attached to the manifold effects of this differentiated principle of foreign policy, it meets with no opposition whatever. Nowhere is there such unanimity as on the question of the preservation of the ancient neutral status. In the course of time, the faith in the absolute rightness of permanent neutrality has only deepened.

If Switzerland is to remain true to her inmost self, there is no other way for her than to abide by her neutrality. It is from that unshakable standpoint that she views the various attempts at union which aim at greater security and welfare for the world. Switzerland regards them in part with sympathy, in part with reserve—with sympathy because the Swiss feel that they cannot confine themselves to their own affairs, that today more than ever they are part of an indivisible world, morally, culturally, and economically. European civilization, born of the fusion of classical antiquity and Christianity, is valid for Switzerland too, is a spiritual heritage she too must defend, a spiritual attitude which implies obligations. The fundamental concepts of European politics, the effort to establish a harmonious balance between the needs of the individual and those of the community, are ideal aims which Switzerland acknowledges too. A country so small in size and so poor in raw materials, with so highly developed an industry, is deeply involved in and dependent on the world economic process. Switzerland is fully aware that she is part of Europe and the world, and that she is therefore one with the other nations in fortune or misfortune. The Swiss is equally far removed from the idolization of his own country as from an internationalism which has lost its roots in patriotism. He is a sincere believer in ultimate peace among the nations. The greatest of Swiss poets wrote :

> The man who cast that hope away,
> And wilfully renounced his faith,
> Had best ne'er seen the light of day,
> For living, life to him is death.

It is not that Switzerland's armed neutrality prevents her from participation in supernational aims. On the contrary, neutrality, properly understood, stands high above mere national egoism. The ideal character of our neutrality is a product of its practical aims. The national instrument of neutrality may do essential service in the realization of supernational aims, and thus of its very nature predisposes Switzerland to regard international movements with sympathy.

Yet, it must be repeated, with reserve too. It was with surprise, anxiety, and in the end pain, that people in Switzerland watched the new world organization of UNO, on which so many hopes of peace had been founded, become the arena of conflicting concepts of the state and political blocs. If UNO, as it proclaimed, was really to guarantee world security and peace, why should individual countries repeatedly endeavour to find support in each other and to form closer unions ? If Switzerland were to join one or other of these groups, she would inevitably be involved in the disputes between the Powers. And that is precisely what she has always avoided and will always avoid.

Yet the world at large still wonders why Switzerland does not at any rate join the Council of Europe, which aims at a federation of Europe on a predominantly cultural basis. It cannot be denied that the goal of the Council of Europe coincides, up to a point, with the inner principles of Swiss growth, namely, federalism and supernationalism. Like Europe, Switzerland consisted for a long time of a loose congeries of states, which lacked political and economic institutions. Just as in present-day Europe, the movement towards closer union originated with a few far-sighted men and private associations, and took time to realize its political aims. And like Europe, Switzerland is not united by race, religion or culture. The Swiss nation, formed by a conscious act, is founded on common historical experience and a general consent to the republican and democratic way of life. When, in the middle of the 19th century, Switzerland became united in a federal state, the modern nationalistic movement was setting in in central Europe. But while, in the old established national states, there was an almost complete coincidence of race, civilization and the state, what rescued Switzerland from the former Holy Roman Empire of the German Nation was simply her supernationalism. Here, as in her liberal constitution, she stood out in contrast to her neighbours and, by her peculiar and independent development, pointed the way to the future, a similar future to that now adumbrated by the Council of Europe. In this way the Swiss Confederation may be described as a prefiguration of the Europe of the future.

But the Swiss are a shrewd, calculating and realistically-minded people. The question in their minds at the moment is whether Europe is ready for closer union, whether a European consciousness really exists at all. Does not the movement represented by the Council of Europe exist only in the minds of a handful of far-sighted men, and is there not a great opposition to it in the public opinion, and among the masses of the people, of all countries? A federation—so the Swiss argument runs—will only preserve peace and prevent war if, as far as possible, it is universal and includes all potential enemies. This is the standpoint from which the Swiss consider the question of representation on the Council of Europe. It must, of course, be pointed out that Switzerland has not yet been invited to join the Council. Efforts have been made to overcome her misgivings by assuring her that membership of the Council would in no way affect her neutrality as established by international law. And it is true that, according to the statutes of the Council of Europe, military matters do not come within its powers. But Swiss neutrality is not merely a status in international law, a legal obligation; it is a principle of foreign policy, a definite attitude towards foreign affairs. The much-quoted Declaration of Neutrality made at Vienna in 1815, and all the similar declarations which preceded and followed it, do not merely establish a status in international law; they also define political aims. It is to be anticipated that, if Switzerland did join the Council of Europe, the maintenance of a strictly neutral foreign policy might become more difficult, if not impossible. Hence a recognition of her neutrality such as she would probably obtain without difficulty would not be of great service to her.

As regards recent movements towards European union, Switzerland has profound misgivings, historical and immediate. Firstly, the Council of Europe does not include the whole of Europe. Further, there is no absolute certainty that the new organization is pursuing only the lofty aims it proclaims. Is its ultimate goal really and exclusively the creation of a united Europe, of a truly European community? The European organization is as yet far from having put its ambitious programme into action even in the economic field. Efforts towards greater freedom in the exchange of goods, the abolition of customs barriers, and the regulation of the currency question, have met with little success so far. It sometimes looks as if the Council of Europe, by its compromises, was falling into line with organizations by means of which Western Europe is endeavouring to protect itself from the East with the help of the United States. Looked at from this realistic standpoint, does not the Council of Europe bear considerable resemblance to the Western Union? Is it not involved in the conflict between East and West? But Switzerland is determined to keep out of all blocs, whether their emphasis is on internal or on foreign affairs, since they would expose her to great dangers. Faithful to her traditional dislike of any involvement in a system of alliances, Switzerland will hold aloof from any policy based on a division of Europe or the world. She will, on the contrary, do all that lies in her power to reconcile enemies and maintain the indivisibility of Europe.

In all likelihood, the question of the representation of Switzerland on the Council of Europe would be put to the federal referendum, optional or compulsory. To judge from what has transpired at public meetings or in the press, a vote at the present moment would certainly have a negative outcome. A refusal to join the Council of Europe would render no good service to the idea of European union. It would therefore be more advisable for the question of Switzerland's membership of the Council to remain open for the present and the answer postponed till later. In the meantime Switzerland's own aims do not run counter to the movement initiated by the Council ; they are on the same lines and even promote it.

For Switzerland is not pursuing a policy of isolation. She desires, now as in the past, to take her part in all movements aiming at a closer union among the nations, cultural, social and economic. She desires to be a mediator between the nations in the intellectual field, and to facilitate communications between them. She strives unceasingly to prevent any recrudescence of national hatreds. She upholds the principles on which international law is founded and supports every effort to bring about peace. This is borne out by the fact that she is a member of a number of technical organizations which have grown up under the leadership of UNO. Thus, she belongs to UNESCO and OEEC. In this connection, deeds speak louder than words. It is not Switzerland's way to throw herself into international activities rashly or impulsively. But if she concludes an agreement, she sticks to it. She prefers active co-operation to endless talk about co-operation. Wherever intellectual or economic interests are at stake, she is an active partner, but refrains from any involvement in the interplay of politics. There she will not co-operate.

Above all, Switzerland wishes to continue her charitable and humanitarian activities. Without any consideration of political feeling, she will help where help is needed. In this way she is able to make her neutrality active and to give it a higher meaning. Switzerland has no reason to fear that she may, through her co-operation in international activities, drift into characterlessness, into watery internationalism. The character of her people is too marked ; they are too deeply rooted in the national soil.

In spite of her neutrality, Switzerland can do such work because her neutrality is not temporary and occasional but permanent. It must be repeated that Swiss neutrality is an element of security in the vicissitudes of international politics. It is just because Switzerland has given the status of permanency to her neutrality, and therefore maintains an unchanging attitude towards foreign affairs, that she can reject the charge of time-serving. (Unlike the occasional neutrals, she bears the heavy burdens of her armed neutrality without any thought of profiting by political power groupings). Not so very long ago she gave fresh proof of her lack of interest in more territory or power by refusing to consider the entrance of the Vorarlberg into the Confederation after the second world war. It is just because Swiss neutrality is neither opportunist nor indifferent that it is able to make a serious contribution to European peace, and to the reconciliation of a world rent by conflicting ideologies. For Swiss neutrality rests on the unconditional respect of treaties and excludes war as a political instrument.

As a consequence of the essential nature of permanent neutrality, the Swiss attitude is quite compatible with an organization for international law and peace. She can exercise important functions in a world founded on law and justice and can participate in the organs of international organization. The efforts of the Confederation to preserve peace will be the more effective the more resolutely she continues to abstain from involvement in any war. Not in spite of, but because of her permanent neutrality, Switzerland can render great services to an international peace organization.

The size and power of Switzerland seem to stand in indirect ratio to the tasks implied in her neutrality. Yet it has been said that that neutrality is moribund. We, on the contrary, regard it as a living force and believe it capable of very important developments. The neutrality of Switzerland rests on the one hand on the determination to preserve the national independence by avoiding all political or military commitments abroad which might entail participation in an armed conflict or adherence to a bloc. It rests on the other hand on the real and profound conviction of international solidarity. Even in face of international relations established by treaty, the principle of the Swiss in foreign affairs will continue to be : " Neutrality and solidarity," that is, the preservation of the national independence and international co-operation for the establishment of lasting peace. The greatest of Swiss poets, who was himself a fiery patriot and a convinced cosmopolitan, once wrote : " Respect every man's country, but love your own."

APPENDIX

Acte portant reconnaissance et garantie de la neutralité perpétuelle de la Suisse et de l'inviolabilité de son Territoire.

L'accession de là Suisse à la Déclaration donnée à Vienne le vingt Mars mil huit cent quinze par les Puissances signataires du Traité de Paris ayant été duement notifiée aux Ministres des Cours Impériales et Royales par l'Acte de la Diète Helvétique du vingt-sept Mai suivant, rien ne s'opposait à ce que l'Acte de la reconnaissance et de la garantie de la neutralité perpétuelle de la Suisse dans ses nouvelles frontières fût fait conformément à la Déclaration susdite. Mais les Puissances ont jugé convenable de suspendre jusqu'à ce jour la signature de cet Acte à cause des changements que les évènements de la guerre et les arrangements qui devaient en être la suite pouvaient apporter aux limites de la Suisse, et des modifications qui pouvaient aussi en résulter dans les dispositions relatives au territoire associé au bienfait de la neutralité du Corps Helvétique.

Ces changements se trouvant déterminés par les stipulations du Traité de Paris de ce jour, les Puissances signataires de la Déclaration de Vienne du 20 Mars font par le présent Acte une reconnaissance formelle et authentique de la neutralité perpétuelle de la Suisse, et Elles lui garantissent l'intégrité et l'inviolabilité de son territoire dans ses nouvelles limites, telles qu'elles sont fixées tant par l'acte du Congrès de Vienne que par le Traité de Paris de ce jour et telles qu'elles le seront ultérieurement : conformément à la disposition du Protocole du trois Novembre, ci-joint en extrait, qui stipule en faveur du Corps Helvétique un nouvel accroissement de territoire à prendre sur la Savoie pour arrondir et désenclaver le Canton de Genève.

Les Puissances reconnaissent et garantissent également la neutralité des parties de la Savoie désignées par l'Acte du Congrès de Vienne du 29 Mars mil huit cent quinze et par le Traité de Paris de ce jour, comme devant jouir de la neutralité de la Suisse, de la même manière que si elles appartenaient à celle-ci.

Les Puissances signataires de la Déclaration du 20 Mars reconnaissent authentiquement par le présent Acte que la neutralité et l'inviolabilité de la Suisse et son indépendance de toute influence étrangère sont dans les vrais intérets de la politique de l'Europe entière.

Elles déclarent qu'aucune induction défavorable aux droits de la Suisse relativement à sa neutralité et à l'inviolabilité de son territoire, ne peut ni ne doit être tirée des évènements qui ont amené le passage des troupes alliées sur une partie du sol Helvétique. Ce passage librement consenti par les Cantons dans la Convention du 20 Mai a été le résultat nécessaire de l'adhésion franche de la Suisse aux principes manifestés par les Puissances signataires du Traité d'alliance du 25 Mars.

Les Puissances se plaisent à reconnaître que la conduite de la Suisse dans cette circonstance d'épreuve a montré qu'elle savait faire de grands sacrifices au bien général et au soutien d'une cause que toutes les Puissances de l'Europe ont défendue et qu'enfin la Suisse est digne d'obtenir les avantages qui lui sont assurés, soit par les dispositions du Congrès de Vienne, soit par le Traité de Paris de ce jour, soit par le présent Acte, auquel toutes les Puissances de l'Europe sont invitées à accéder.

En foi de quoi la présente Déclaration a été faite et signée à Paris le vingt Novembre de l'an de gràce mil huit cent quinze.

THE END

GEORGE ALLEN & UNWIN LTD
LONDON: 40 MUSEUM STREET, W.C.1
CAPE TOWN: 58–60 LONG STREET
SYDNEY, N.S.W.: 55 YORK STREET
TORONTO: 91 WELLINGTON STREET WEST
CALCUTTA: 17 CENTRAL AVE., P.O. DHARAMTALA
BOMBAY: 15 GRAHAM ROAD, BALLARD ESTATE
WELLINGTON, N.Z.: 8 KINGS CRESCENT, LOWER HUTT